SPIRITS OF INITIATION

Spirits of Initiation

A Study of the Toys of Dionysos

H. Jeremiah Lewis

Nysa Press

Cover art:
Wayne and Mark Made Me.
panfineart.com

Spirits of Initiation
Copyright © 2015 by H. Jeremiah Lewis

All rights reserved. No part of this book may be reproduced by any means or in any form whatsoever without written permission from the author, except for brief quotations embodied in literary articles or reviews.

Fragment from Aischylos' *Isthmiastai* or *Theoroi*

Satyr: Don't confuse us with your verbal wiles and foreign proverbs!

Dionysos: Oh, you'd rather hide behind a shield and utter words against me that are out of order – that I am no good at fighting with iron, that I'm a cowardly, effeminate being who doesn't belong among males. And now you make these further, fresh accusations, more vile than any of your previous insults, and you slander both me and the choral festival for which I am assembling a multitude. No one, young or old, willingly abandons the two rows of my chorus, yet you are Isthmiizing, garlanding yourselves with pine branches and not paying ivy its due honor at all. For this you'll shed tears but it won't be because you've got smoke in your eyes!

Satyr: No, I will never depart from the sanctuary! Why do you keep threatening me like this? In response I call on Poseidon of the Isthmus. He will protect me….

Dionysos: Since you are set on learning these new ways, I've brought you some new Toys, freshly fashioned on the adze and the anvil. This, here, is the first of the playthings for you.

Satyr: Not me! Give it to one of my friends.

Dionysos: Don't refuse, my good fellow, just because of a bad vibration. Accept these gifts which I bestow upon you.

Dionysos hands the Toy to the Satyr.

Satyr: What pleasure is to be had of this? What am I even supposed to do with it?

Dionysos: It suits your new profession.

Satyr: But what do I do with it exactly? I don't like this thing, it confounds me!

Dionysos: You play the game. Everybody's doing it.

THIS BOOK IS DEDICATED TO THE MAD AND HUNGRY ONES,
INITIATORS OF THE STARRY BULL,
AND TO ALL THOSE THEY HAVE TOUCHED.

Contents

Foreword: They Will Change You 1
Opening Remarks 3
Why Is the Starry Bull Strain of Bacchic Orphism So Horrific? 6
The Bloody Heart of Our Mysteries: *Sparagmos* and *Omophagia* 11
Some Background on the Toys of Dionysos 23

THE TOYS
Sphaira the Ball 44
Astragaloi the Dice 51
Trochos the Wheel 59
Rhombos the Bullroarer 67
Strobilos the Top 71
Krotala the Rattle 78
Paignia Kampesiguia the Puppet 92
Pókos the Tuft of Wool 103
Mela the Golden Apples 121
Esoptron the Mirror 134

About the Author 149
Also from Nysa Press 150

Foreword: They Will Change You

A couple years ago I was traveling around the east coast of Australia living as a vagabond, camping out or staying in an assortment of hotels and motels, exploring and making art along the way. One night after consuming some sort of *substance* I found myself in one of those rundown 1970s road motels staring at a mirror. I was contemplating the death of Dionysos Zagreus, how it is the mirror that captures him through his own reflection. His own identity. And how this is what leads to his death.

Then something began to happen to me. Something strange. I don't know if I can really articulate it, but as I looked at my reflection I began seeing myself through the eyes of my counter self. Like my consciousness was transferred to the reflective world beyond the mirror, transferred to the *other side*. To this day I still don't know if I have returned.

That was my first experience with one of the Toys of Dionysos, Esoptron. A single, simple encounter that has profoundly changed my life forever. Under Sannion's tutelage I've been exposed to every Toy of Dionysos, each "gifting" some sort of life-altering epiphany. Each changing my perception of what we term "reality."

And this is where I'll offer a word of caution. Once you let the Toys into your life you will undergo a transformation. For some, this could be undesirable, frightening even. Like Dionysos, these Toys will force you to question yourself, they will strip your identity down and remould it into something new. Depending on your own perspective this can be for better or worse.

So what exactly are the Toys of Dionysos? You'll discover that through the contents of this book, but let me say you already know them. They are in every literal sense childhood Toys. Yet, also something we fear the most. It is no coincidence that they are often featured in horror films, literature, music, art, even video games. They are objects that we innately know and understand, but unlocking their secrets is where the fun begins.

As a final word I'd like to say that I'm deeply honoured to introduce this book and also co-create the cover art. These Toys have taught me so much and, I dare say, aided me in becoming who I am today.

Play nice,
Markos Gage
Dionysian Artist

Opening Remarks

Contained within these pages are the Toys of Dionysos as we work with them in the Starry Bull tradition.

But what are they?

They are living symbols, a collective of intelligent forces which oversee and embody the processes of initiation and personal transformation. Not quite gods, and yet vastly more than men; *daimones* as the Greeks would say, spirits in the common parlance.

This much I am certain of when it comes to them: they are old and strange and feral and they would be far more dangerous if they were not obedient to the will of Dionysos. Even so they should be approached with caution and the utmost deference. It is their job to test and hone those who belong to Dionysos, and they are very, very good at it. Often they will employ deceit, trickery and disguise to do so – or simply for their own amusement. Consequently there is very little concerning their origin or nature that I take at face value. I am not bothered by this inherent ambiguity because their results speak volumes: I would not be half the Dionysian I am today without their assistance, nor am I alone in reaping the benefits of a relationship with the Toys. But I'm also not stupid, like the frog who expects the scorpion to behave contrary to who he is.

And never forget: the Toys started out as adversaries, terrible weapons used against Dionysos.

Who made them? Did Hera conceive them in her devastating wrath or were they forged by the Kyklopes like the mighty thunderbolts of Zeus? Or perhaps the Daktyloi, the Telchines, the Kabeiroi or another group of primitive wizard-smiths (who in some versions of the myth are stand-ins for the "Titans") are responsible for calling them into being? Could they belong to the generation of the rebellious Kronos and the Melian nymphs? Are they even older still? Perhaps they did not exist until people started writing about them.

Nothing in the sources says, nor has anything they've shown myself or others cleared this mystery up.

All we know is that they were the means by which the young god was distracted and tragically dismembered.

Was this an attack or a rite of passage? Were they separate beings or mere objects or animistically the spirits-within-objects? Did they act of their own free will or were they under compulsion? What did they do to him, put him through, make him experience? Was this the first time they were employed so? How did they come to switch sides? Did they consume Dionysos, only to be converted from within? Did he return from the dead and overpower them?

So many questions without answers.

All we know is that afterwards they start showing up in Bacchic Orphic contexts, accruing complex bodies of symbolic value (which I will detail for you over the next hundred-and-forty pages or so) and now they are here (especially, though not just, for those of us who are adherents of the Starry Bull tradition), helping us to learn and grow and reach our full potential as Dionysians.

Why? What do they get out of the bargain?

I could offer little more than speculation, but I'll tell you this: whatever they ask it is worth it, and then some.

In this book's companion I share more of my personal experiences with and insights about the Toys of Dionysos as well as how to begin a working relationship with them. I provide exercises, practices and recommend devotional activities that have proven successful not just for myself but a number of students I have introduced to the Toys of Dionysos over the years. I discuss how to encounter them through meditation, dreams, altered states and ritual as well as how to utilize them for divination, healing, cleansing, protection and other things that conventionally fall under the rubric of magic. It is a much more "hands on" sort of book than this one, and necessarily so.

I have separated the material so that each book could serve its own specific function unimpeded. Herein is contained all that is known about the Toys' mythology, symbolism and history. Beyond the educational purpose of collecting this information, each Toy's section can be read devotionally as a means of focusing the mind upon them and calling the Toys forth. The readings are densely packed with sources and little in the way of commentary; this is so that you can let your mind wander in whatever circuitous routes it pleases and draw your own conclusions about the Toys, without undue influence from me. Let yourself boldly leap to wild conclusions, regardless of what another might think. No matter how much you absorb, there will always be new things to discover and new connections to be made. To do this you have to really spend time with the text, and unfortunately when the readings were combined with the more practical material people would just rush through to get to the meat and bones and thus not receive the full benefit of serious reflection. Hence the division.

And finally, don't be afraid to take copious notes and scribble stuff in the margins; this book is meant to be used and if it gets too trashed you can always purchase another copy!

H. Jeremiah Lewis aka Sannion,
at the Heart of the Labyrinth,
on the 11th of November, 2015 CE

Why Is the Starry Bull Strain of Bacchic Orphism So Horrific?

The Toys of Dionysos are the holders of the mysteries of the Starry Bull tradition, so it seems appropriate to say a few words about this tradition and its rather unconventional mythology before we get started.

To be blunt, Starry Bull mythology is horrific. No one contests this. Its central figure is a god who was torn apart as an infant or a young man in his prime, and this deed was performed either by the divine figures who had been appointed to guard him or the women most devoted to him. This god goes on to suffer madness and mockery and many of his closest circle are violently persecuted. His prophets are imprisoned, tortured and torn to pieces. Many of his women are suicides, with hanging being the commonest cause of death. He brings healing, release and justice to the victims of unthinkably terrible crimes. He leads his retinue of frenzied spirits in the hunt and rules a portion of hell.

This is the stuff of nightmares. Who in their right mind would worship such a god? And for that matter how can one claim that this is an accurate portrayal of Dionysos, the mirthful lord of wine and freedom?

It isn't meant to be.

The Starry Bull tradition is a modern expression of a strain of Bacchic Orphism, itself but one of the many forms that the religion of Dionysos took in antiquity. This influences both the choice of source material that we draw upon and even more importantly how that material is interpreted. At no time do we deny that there are other faces which the god may show his devotees, nor that there are other avenues which open unto him. On the contrary, the beliefs and practices which shape the Starry Bull tradition are best seen as supplementary to more conventional forms of religiosity, with the tension between them a necessary component.

Let me explain what I mean by way of an example. Meet Hermagenes, son of Dolion of the Oineis tribe, a fairly average middle child born into a moderately well-off family in the Athens of Demetrios Poliorketes. Considering the tumultuous times he finds himself in, Hermagenes is not an ambitious man and uses the leisure provided by his father's estate to devote himself primarily to religious and social endeavors. Not only does he maintain cultus for the gods of his household and honor his illustrious ancestors as he was raised from infancy to do, but unlike a lot of his contemporaries he devotes himself to the gods and heroes of his *deme* and *phyle*. He has an important role in several of the larger civic festivals, belongs to a couple religious guilds and observes their calendars of monthly sacrifices, has served as *choregos* and *gymnasiarch* in the past, visits a specialist in Orphic rites once a month for purifications, attends lectures in Platonic theology at the Academy, and goes to the various temples strewn throughout his city when the need arises. He has made pilgrimage to Delphi, Eleusis and Samothrace, and also received initiation into the mysteries of Meter, Pan, Sabazios and two separate Bacchic cults.

All of these various threads, together, weave the tapestry of Hermagenes' religious life. No one of them is more important than the others, though each provide him with different benefits and make different demands on his time, resources and mental energy.

Ideally things should be no different today. An adherent of the Starry Bull tradition is free to honor as many other gods and spirits as they are called to, and even to honor the members of our loose pantheon in different forms and through different ways alongside their Starry Bull practice. This is not just permitted, it is strongly encouraged.

After all, this tradition was never intended to be all things for all people. We have carved off a small portion of that which is Dionysian for our own and intend to explore it to the fullest. It is a fragment and cannot provide you with all you need for a full and rich religious life any more than eating only grapes and figs will lead to a whole and healthy existence.

Our piece is bloody and trembling, and that's why it's ours.

You see, we aren't well. No one in this fucked up society is, but unlike the majority we recognize this all-important fact about ourselves. We each come to this path with different ailments of different degrees of severity but our common bond is madness. Madness that can be cured by the god, and madness that is sent by him. All the greatest blessings of the gods may arrive by way of madness, but madness will also destroy you if you let it. And so we learn to dance with our madness. Instead of hiding from it, locking it away, suppressing it until it morphs into something far more dangerous, we let it out to play, try it on like a costume, see all the beautiful and ugly things it has to show us about the world, and about ourselves.

In a walnut shell, that's what the Starry Bull tradition is. It's giving yourself permission to go a little mad sometimes, to look at things through insane eyes.

Why? Isn't madness bad for individuals and communities?

Sure, but so is not making space for madness. In fact, far more social ills stem from repression than cutting loose.

Think about how much we lose by being divided and in conflict with ourselves.

When was the last time you played with finger paints? When was the last time you sang or danced, regardless of who might be around? When was the last time you ate something just because it tasted good and fuck the calories? When was the last time you just walked or drove in a random direction, with nowhere particular to be? When was the last time you plaited a flower crown or hugged a tree? When was the last time you cried at a movie? When was the last time you screamed or broke something because you were angry – or even better, when you weren't? When was the last time you felt truly alive?

Judging by the prevalence of zombies and convention-breaking anti-heroes in pop culture, I'm guessing not for a while. These tropes wouldn't have the appeal they do if folks were living vital and authentic lives. But that's really hard to do at the dawn of the 21st century in the West. From the cradle we're bombarded with messages carefully crafted to keep us complacent, conformist, unhappy, and striving to meet impossible and contradictory standards that wouldn't even be fulfilling if we could. And the really fucked up thing is that this conditioning is so pervasive and runs so deep within us that even if you choose not to buy into it and are a pretty introspective and conscientious soul you've still got issues in need of working out. Some of them are just part and parcel of the human condition. Hell, even chimps have anxiety disorders.

And that's why the Starry Bull tradition is such a horror show.

This shit's buried deep, deep down inside us and if you want to root it out you're going to need more than to just lie on some dude's couch and talk at him for an hour.

Terror, hunger, savagery, disgust – real primal emotions that get the heart racing and blood pumping – these things help you step out of your small, conditioned self and cleanse the wounds of ages past. You must descend into the abyss if you would attain catharsis; then and only then are you able to rise up in wholeness and joy. There is no true freedom that you have not suffered for.

And yet there's something else, a subtler and in some ways more important process that goes along with this. The reconciliation of opposites, through which we discover the true nature of things, ourselves included. A small portion of man rises above the surface, like the barest tip of the iceberg – and he mistakes this for his personality. All the dreams and fears and fantasies and cravings that he does not associate with himself, considers unreal, unacceptable, inconsequential and does his damndest to lock up and never let see the light of day – those things don't just go away. They become twisted, sick or withered to nothing. Either he becomes psychically impotent or lashes out unexpectedly, irrationally and violently, destroying all he's worked so hard to build up. Why? Because he cannot reconcile his notions of himself as a "good" person with the monstrous urges he feels, because he's running from the pain and disappointment in his past. And he rips apart the whole world in the same fashion, seeing things as pure and filthy, desirable and repugnant, heavenly and diabolical, rational and mad.

Most things are not one or the other – they're both, and more, and our horrible mythology forces us to confront that artificial dichotomy and every other false notion we've got rattling around in our heads.

Like that the world's fair and nothing bad ever happens to good people.

Our god was ripped to bloody shreds and the ones who loved him most did it!

Fucking let that sink in for a second – even the gods can suffer affliction. Makes what you're going through kinda small potatoes, huh? And yet here's the great part. The god who has suffered most in this tragic fucking universe wants only for us to be happy. To him, what you're going through isn't tiny and irrelevant. He suffers through it along with you, and rejoices in your triumph.

That's why we focus so much on gruesome and bizarre stories of violence, madness and sex. We do not flinch from seeing the worst in our gods and spirits because they have earned our trust and our devotion and what's more because we are driven by passionate longing to know them in their entirety, without judgment or expectation. And if you can look at a god with that kind of pure, unconditional love what's stopping you from seeing yourself that way too? From that comes the most important freedom – the freedom to truly be you. Once you know who you are and what you're capable of you can wear any mask you want and reveal only select portions of yourself to the world as the situation requires without the risk of losing yourself or becoming what you pretend.

But not everyone needs that, or needs it all the time. The Starry Bull tradition makes no exclusive demands – indeed, for every story we put forth, we put forth another in contradistinction to it. And another, and another. Because it's the story behind the stories and the way those stories are told that defines our tradition. Understanding comes through comparison, which necessitates something other than the Starry Bull. Which is why most of our members are involved in numerous other communities and religious traditions as well.

If all of that doesn't make sense, don't worry, it wasn't meant for you. If it does, you probably *should* worry as you're on your way to becoming one of us.

Who are you?

Why, you're a mix of mud and stars, with blood of the Titans in your veins, a devotee of the mad god. And don't you ever forget it.

The Bloody Heart of Our Mysteries: *Sparagmos* and *Omophagia*

Wikipedia describes what many people consider to be the central myth of the Orphics:

> Zeus had intended Zagreus to be his heir, but a jealous Hera persuaded the Titans to kill the child. Like the infant Zeus in Cretan myth, the child Zagreus was entrusted to the Titans who distracted him with toys. While he gazed into a mirror they tried to seize him and he fled, changing into various animal forms in his attempt to escape. Finally he took the form of a bull, and in that form they caught him, tore him to pieces, and devoured him. Zeus, discovering the crime, hurled a thunderbolt at the Titans, turning them to ashes, but Persephone (or in some accounts Athena, Rhea, or Hermes) managed to recover Zagreus' heart. From the ashes of the Titans, mixed with the divine flesh they had eaten, came humankind; this explains the mix of good and evil in humans, the story goes, for humans possess both a trace of divinity as well as the Titans' maliciousness.

Lovely story, isn't it?

Problem is, that is *not* the Orphic myth – technically speaking it's not even *an* Orphic myth. What you're reading is a modern reconstruction that combines two originally separate mythic threads and is based entirely on a single source, a complex alchemical analogy made by the Alexandrian philosopher Olympiodoros in the 6th century CE:

> And the mythical argument is as such: four reigns are told of in the Orphic tradition. The first is that of Ouranos, to which Kronos succeeds after cutting off the genitals of his father. After Kronos, Zeus becomes king, having hurled his father down into Tartaros. Then Dionysos succeeds Zeus. Through the scheme of Hera, they say, his retainers, the Titans, tear him to pieces and eat his flesh. Zeus, angered by the deed, blasts them with his thunderbolts, and from the sublimate of the vapors that rise from them comes the matter from which men are created. Therefore we must not kill ourselves, not because, as the text appears to say, we are in the body as a kind of shackle, for that is obvious, and Socrates would not call this a mystery; but we must not kill ourselves because our bodies are Dionysiac; we are, in fact, a part of him, if indeed we come about from the sublimate of the Titans who ate his flesh. (*Commentary on the Phaedrus* 1.3)

Up until his time there was a myth about the dismemberment of Dionysos Zagreus (often, though not always, as part of the succession of divine kingship) and there was a myth that mankind had sprung from the blood of the Titans or Giants spilled in their battle with the Gods, but in no way were these two events connected.

Consider the following:

> Then the son from his ambush stretched forth his left hand and in his right took the great long sickle with jagged teeth, and swiftly lopped off his own father's members and cast them away to fall behind him. And not vainly did they fall from his hand; for all the bloody drops that gushed forth Gaia received, and as the seasons moved round she bare the strong Erinyes and the great Gigantes with gleaming armor, holding long spears in their hands and the Nymphai whom they call Meliai all over the boundless earth. And so soon as he had cut off the members with flint and cast them from the land into the surging sea, they were swept away over the main a long time: and a white foam spread around them from the immortal flesh, and in it there grew the maiden Aphrodite. (Hesiod, *Theogony* 147–187)

> There they lay, grim broken bodies crushed in huge collapse, and Terra, drenched in her children's weltering blood, gave life to that warm gore; and to preserve memorial of her sons refashioned it in human form. But that new stock no less despised the gods and relished cruelty, bloodshed and outrage – born beyond doubt of blood. (Ovid, *Metamorphoses* 1.151)

Zeus the father made a third age of mortals, this time of bronze, not at all like the silver one. Fashioned from ash trees, they were dreadful and mighty and bent on the harsh deeds of war and violence; they ate no bread and their hearts were strong as adamant. (Hesiod, *Works and Days* 143–147)

The Pelasgians who drew the root of their race from the blood of the Sithonian Giants. (Lycophron, *Alexandra* 1358)

All mankind, we are all from the blood of the Titans. Thus, because they were the enemies of the gods and fought against them, we are not beloved by the gods either, but we are punished by them and we are born into retribution, being in custody in this life for a certain time as long as we each live ... This harsh and foul-aired prison, which we call the cosmos, has been prepared by the gods. (Dio Chrysostom, *Oration* 30, 10–11)

Not a mention of Dionysos Zagreus anywhere.

Likewise when we read accounts of his dismemberment there's nothing about mankind's generation from blood or ash:

The stories told of Dionysos by the people of Patrai, that he was reared in Mesatis in Achaia and incurred there all sorts of perils through the plots of the Titanes. (Pausanias, *Description of Greece* 7.19.4)

This god was born in Crete, men say, of Zeus and Persephone, and Orpheus has handed down the tradition in the initiatory rites that he was torn in pieces by the Titanes. (Diodoros Sikeliotes, *Library of History* 5.75.4)

To soften the transports of their tyrant's rage, the Cretans made the day of the death into a religious festival, and founded a yearly rite with a triennial dedication, performing in order all that the child in his death both did and suffered. They tore a live bull with their teeth, recalling the cruel feast in their annual commemoration, and by uttering dissonant cries through the depths of the forest they imitated the ravings of an unbalanced mind, in order that it might be believed that the awful crime was committed not by guile but in madness. Before them was borne the chest in which the sister secretly stole away the heart, and with the sound of flutes and the clashing of cymbals they imitated the rattles with which the boy was deceived. Thus to do honor to a tyrant an obsequious rabble has made a god out of one who was not able to find burial. (Firmicus Maternus, *The Error of Pagan Religion* 6.5)

According to Terpander of Lesbos, Dionysos, who is sometimes called Sabazios, was nursed by Nysa; he was the son of Zeus and Persephone and was eventually torn in pieces by the Titans. (Johannes Lydus, *On the Months* 72)

The mysteries of Dionysos are wholly inhuman; for while still a child, and the Curetes danced around his cradle clashing their weapons, and the Titans having come upon them by stealth, and having beguiled him with childish toys, these very Titans tore him limb from limb when but a child, as the bard of this mystery, the Thracian Orpheus, says: "Cone, and spinning-top, and limb-moving doll, and fair golden apples from the clear-toned Hesperides." And the useless symbols of this mystic rite it will not be useless to exhibit for condemnation. These are dice, ball, hoop, apples, top, looking-glass, tuft of wool. Athene, to resume our account, having abstracted the heart of Dionysos received the name Pallas from its palpitating (*pallein*). And the Titans who had torn him limb from limb, setting a caldron on a tripod, and throwing into it the members of Dionysos, first boiled them down, and then fixing them on spits, "held them over the fire." But Zeus having appeared, since he was a god, having speedily perceived the savor of the pieces of flesh that were being cooked, that savor which your gods agree to have assigned to them as their perquisite, assails the Titans with his thunderbolt, and consigns the members of Dionysos to his son Apollo to be interred. And he – for he did not disobey Zeus – bore the dismembered corpse to Parnassus, and there deposited it. (Clement of Alexandria, Book Two of *Exhortation to the Greeks*)

Dionysos was deceived by the Titans, and fell (ἐκπίπτοντος) from the throne of Zeus, and was torn in pieces by them, and his remains being afterwards put together again, he returned as it were to life, and ascended into heaven? (Origen, *Contra Celsum* 4.17)

A significant number of sources on his dismemberment make it clear that Zagreus was not always envisioned as a child when this terrible event took place:

The one who greatly hunts, as the writer of the *Alcmeonis* said "Mistress Earth, and Zagreus highest of all the gods." That is, Dionysos. (*Etymologicum Gudianum* s.v. Zagreus)

Some writers of myth, however, relate that there was a second Dionysos who was much earlier in time than the one we have just mentioned. For according to them there was born of Zeus and Persephone a Dionysos who is called by some Sabazios and whose birth and sacrifices and honors are celebrated at night and in secret, because of the disgraceful conduct which is a consequence of the gatherings. They state also that he excelled in sagacity and was the first to attempt the yoking of oxen and by their aid to effect the sowing of the seed, this being the reason why they also represent him as wearing a horn. (Diodoros Sikeliotes, *Library of History* 4.4.1)

After Juno observed that his son, ignoble and born of a concubine, ruled such a great kingdom, she saw to it that he should be killed while hunting, and encouraged the Titans to drive his father Jove from the kingdom and restore it to Saturn. When they tried to mount to heaven, Jove with the help of Minerva, Apollo, and Diana, cast them headlong into Tartarus. On Atlas, who had been their leader, he put the vault of the sky; even now he is said to hold up the sky on his shoulders. (Hyginus, *Fabulae* 150)

Furthermore, so that we might seem to go more deeply, the story says that the Giants found Bacchus inebriated. After they tore him to pieces limb by limb, they buried the bits, and a little while later he arose alive and whole. We read that the disciples of Orpheus interpreted this fiction philosophically and that they represent this story in his sacred rites. (*The Third Vatican Mythographer* 12.5)

In one variant tradition Dionysos actually defeated the Titans in battle and became their king:

> The struggle having proved sharp and many having fallen on both sides, Kronos finally was wounded and victory lay with Dionysos, who had distinguished himself in the battle. Thereupon the Titans fled to the regions which had once been possessed by Ammon, and Dionysos gathered up a multitude of captives and returned to Nysa. Here, drawing up his force in arms about the prisoners, he brought a formal accusation against the Titans and gave them every reason to suspect that he was going to execute the captives. But when he got them free from the charges and allowed them to make their choice either to join him in his campaign or to go scot free, they all chose to join him, and because their lives had been spared contrary to their expectation they venerated him like a god. Dionysos, then, taking the captives singly and giving them a libation of wine, required of all of them an oath that they would join in the campaign

without treachery and fight manfully until death. (Diodoros Sikeliotes, *Library of History* 3.71.4–6)

A clue that the generation of man from the residue of the Titans and the dismemberment of Zagreus cannot be linked in this way is made clear by the tradition that Zeus used the preserved heart of his first son to create his second by impregnating Semele with it:

> Liber, son of Jove and Proserpina, was dismembered by the Titans, and Jove gave his heart, torn to bits, to Semele in a drink. When she was made pregnant by this, Juno changing herself to look like Semele's nurse, Beroe, said to her, "Daughter, ask Jove to come to you as he comes to Juno, so you may know what pleasure it is to sleep with a god." At her suggestion Semele made this request of Jove, and was smitten by a thunderbolt. (Hyginus, *Fabulae* 167)

When did Semele live? Not at the infancy of man – her father was a Phoenician immigrant who settled in Thebes and became king there. Chronologically, Herodotos (*Histories* 2.145.1) places Agenor the father of Kadmos circa 2000 BCE, so people had already been around for quite some time at that point.

But the real reason that it's important to disentangle this thread of myth is because it obscures the true function of Dionysos within Orphism, which can be summed up by this quote from the *Orationes* of Aelius Aristides:

> Nothing can be so firmly bound, neither by illness, nor by wrath or fortune, that cannot be released by Dionysos.

The *aition* for this function is found in the story of Melinoë. You see, the goddess Melinoë was conceived when Zeus disguised himself as Haides and violently raped his daughter Persephone, mangling her flesh in the process. The wound grew into rage and that rage became personified as Melinoë who was transformed from a wrathful Fury into a gentle goddess when Dionysos Eubouleos was willing to sit and listen to her tell her story, as he had listened and thereby soothed the vengeful anger of Hephaistos when no one else would. Subsequently Melinoë became a fierce protector of his initiates as well as the rejected and forgotten dead – and that lies at the heart of Dionysos' role within Orphism.

And yet that is not to say that the dismemberment of Dionysos is unimportant within our tradition – for me it has been hugely important and has had far-reaching implications in my personal life. As just one instance, because of it I am no longer a vegetarian. How can one be a Bacchic Orphic and not be a vegetarian, you may be asking? Pretty easily, as it turns out.

If you read accounts of Orphism by the likes of Thomas Taylor, Jane Ellen Harrison and W. K. Guthrie, it seems like they were a reformist Protestant sect that espoused pacifism, celibacy, teetotalism, vegetarianism and an escape from *metempsychosis* (transmigration of souls) through spiritual enlightenment. But if you pick up any decent contemporary study on Orphism you'll find at least one chapter devoted to the shifting trends within Orphic studies. Jesus, have people come to some wild conclusions about these guys, most of which radically contradict each other. It's quite amusing, really – plus we can all use periodic reminders that the mere fact that someone in academia has said something does not make it true.

The reason that there's so much confusion, I believe, is because there was never an ancient Orphic church, a set of universal doctrines or myth, or even really an Orphic movement for that matter. What we've got are a lot of individuals, and sometimes small, isolated groups, who attach authority to the name of Orpheus, many of whom attributed their own writings and rituals to him. This process began around the 6th century BCE and continued more or less until the closing of the Platonic Academy by Justinian. (There was also some Christian and Renaissance pseudoepigraphica though this is quite outside the bounds of any discernibly Orphic tradition. Little can be said with certainty about the historical Thracian arch-poet and founder of mysteries, but I think it's a safe bet to say that Orpheus was *not* a crypto-monotheist who prophesied the coming of Jesus.)

Although we've come a long way in our understanding of the ancient Orphics you still find a lot of people holding on to these outdated notions, especially with regard to their supposed vegetarianism. There are some issues (interpretation of the "hard and grievous circle" and how much of the Zagreus myth was known, and when) where cases can be made in a variety of ways, but I simply do not believe that we can ascribe vegetarianism to them across the board.

To begin with, out of the wealth of material we have on Orpheus and the Orphics (over four hundred pages' worth in the latest collection) there are only a handful of allusions to this, most of which can be explained away by more sensible and straightforward interpretations. (For instance "not to stain one's hands with blood" most likely means "don't commit homicide," especially when you consider the frequent Orphic concern for the removal of pollution associated with murder.)

Furthermore, of the handful of passages which are commonly cited in support of this claim two of them are part of mythological plays, and in those plays context is everything.

The first is a fragment likely contrasting the purity of the chorus with the savage bloodthirstiness of king Minos and his bull, and notably comes after the chorus of initiates discuss their own participation in the Dionysian sacrament of *sparagmós* and *omophagia* (the tearing apart of a live animal and consumption of its raw and still bloody flesh) – so clearly there were times when even these fictive initiates broke their taboo.

> Son of the Phoenician princess, child of Tyrian Europa and great Zeus, ruler over hundred-fortressed Crete — here am I, come from the sanctity of temples roofed with cut beam of our native wood, its true joints of cypress welded together with Chalybean axe and cement from the bull. Pure has my life been since the day when I became an initiate of Idaean Zeus. Where midnight Zagreus roves, I rove; I have endured his thunder-cry; fulfilled his red and bleeding feasts; held the Great Mother's mountain flame; I am set free and named by name a Bakchos of the Mailed Priests. Having all-white garments, I flee the birth of mortals and, not nearing the place of corpses, I guard myself against the eating of ensouled flesh.
> (Euripides, *Cretans* fragment 472)

And in the second play, also by Euripides, Theseus is trying to smear his son Hippolytos (whom he suspects of committing incest) by accusing him of being an overly sensitive, bookish prig who is merely feigning his Orphic piety:

> Are you, then, the companion of the gods, as a man beyond the common? Are you the chaste one, untouched by evil? I will never be persuaded by your vauntings, never be so unintelligent as to impute folly to the gods. Continue then your confident boasting, take up a diet of greens and play the showman with your food, make Orpheus your lord and engage in mystic rites, holding the vaporings of many books in honor. For you have been found out. To all I give the warning: avoid men like this. For they make you their prey with their high-holy-sounding words while they contrive deeds of shame.
> (Euripides, *Hippolytos* 948–957)

Of course what people seem to forget is that none of what Theseus says is accurate – that's the whole point, since he's trying to goad Hippolytos into confessing the role he played in his mother's suicide. Hipploytos, after all, was basically a big dumb jock who got into trouble by spurning the goddess Aphrodite so that he could spend all of his time out in the woods *hunting* with Artemis.

The paucity of information on this is rather telling in light of the fact that there are a bunch of sources written by people who identified themselves as Orphics but didn't say anything at all about such a prohibition. In fact there are a couple lists of wild and domesticated animals, aquatic creatures and vegetables that were denied them on religious grounds which makes you wonder why they'd bother with such specificity if they were to avoid ensouled foods altogether. If this was such a widespread feature it's equally curious that the Orphics aren't mentioned more often in the numerous treatises by philosophers against meat-eating. Likewise, why are some of the most notable Orphics – including the soldier who was cremated with the Derveni papyrus, Queen Olympias and her Makedonian court, a Roman senator, a slave and a gladiator – all known to have consumed flesh? Plus a ton of sources mention Orphics performing sacrifice, including the slaughter of hekatombs and offerings to the ancestors and underworld powers. Old dead things ain't gonna accept animal crackers in substitution!

That's not to say that *all* Orphics did consume flesh. There was a lot of crossover between the Orphic and Pythagorean communities in Magna Graecia and we know that a number of the latter wrote books under Orpheus' name, especially when their political plans fell apart and the neighboring communities began a systematic purge; indeed they may have thought that such duplicity was the only means of preserving their master's teachings. (Though, ironically, it is sometimes claimed that Pythagoras was the first author of *Orphika*.) By and large the Pythagoreans were adherents of *metempsychosis* and vegetarianism (except in the case of soldiers, athletes and others who required a more robust diet; Pythagoras is even said to have sacrificed an ox after making an important mathematical discovery) so when we do see a rare instance of this ascribed to Orpheus and his followers in all probability it's coming from a Pythagorean source who's trying to pass or at least an Orphic who was influenced by the Samian's teachings.

But what really changed my stance on this was my own brush with *sparagmós* and *omophagia*.

So there I was, huddled in a corner, covered in fear sweat and laughing maniacally while tripping balls from eating an heroically large dose of amanita muscaria. That's what someone outside my head would have seen; inside, I was running through the shadowy, winding passages of a labyrinth while terrifying inky creatures with faces bright white from the ash they'd smeared themselves with chased after me. What had me laughing so insanely was that I felt like Dionysos. I could feel the weight of his spirit within me and I had this weird overlay of his thoughts coupled with my own in my head. *And yet Dionysos was the one leading the monsters*, who were getting closer and closer with every panting breath. Eventually they caught me, tore me apart and consumed my flesh beginning with my still-beating heart. Then, once they were finished, Dionysos restored me, stitching my body back together like Frankenstein's monster, except the heart was missing. My chest was an empty cavern, a dry krater. Into this he stuffed his own heart – a clump of ivy with black-green leaves like you find on Apulian vases. Except they were alive, throbbing with vitality and consciousness. Different from our own – older, slower, collective – but real nonetheless. I knew with rock-solid certainty that (among the many other things that act entailed) my god had shown me what life for the ivy, and by extension all plants, was like – a life that he partook of as equally as he did human and animal life. Dionysos is the god of life in all its myriad forms – and he was simultaneously the god of death as well. It was all this elaborate interplay, this sacred dance that blurred the boundaries and in which we both lose and discover ourselves.

Shortly afterwards I stopped being a vegetarian. It was hard; I'd been one since my early teens and it was a huge part of my identity. I always felt a smug superiority to meat-eaters even if I wasn't one of those obnoxious vegetarians who went around giving unsolicited lectures on ethics and the cruelty and wastefulness of feasting on flesh. I quietly ate with people, hoping they would take notice of my pure food and be shamed into adopting a more evolved diet.

What I realized is that I was a hypocrite trying to escape a necessary part of embodied existence, trying to avoid any debt or consequences for my actions. And I did this by willfully ignoring the simple and inescapable fact that I was alive because I was consuming other forms of life.

We're good at weaving excuses to justify our actions and avoid having to examine too deeply beliefs whose implications make us uncomfortable.

It's animal life that matters; they are the only ones who are developed enough to have a nervous system and intelligence enough to suffer and be aware of their suffering. An animal will try to flee in order to escape that suffering and preserve itself – but a plant just sits there, hell some actually *want* to be eaten so that they can disperse their seed through our poo. Why, we're doing them a favor by eating them!

What arrogance! What presumption!

Even if that was true on a species level, how was I to know what an individual plant may have felt about their role in the process? Just because it didn't have the means for fleeing doesn't necessarily mean it didn't want to. And besides, as a poster on reddit said:

> In general, all animals eat living entities. Plants are the only true innocents to do no harm by requiring only soil, air, and sunlight. This means vegans consciously choose to prey on the only living entities to have never harmed another.

If I truly wanted to avoid harming conscious and living entities I wouldn't differentiate between types of consciousness, favoring only those closest to my own – I simply wouldn't eat. Except that would end up harming me and I wasn't yet prepared to die. I had work still to do for my god and for my community. I wanted to serve them, to help ease their suffering and bring joy to them in whatever capacity I could. To do that, I had to put myself first – decide that the preservation of my own life, which enabled me to do good in the world, was important enough that it warranted taking in other life in order to make that happen.

It's as Celsus in the *Alethes Logos* says:

> If in obedience to the traditions of their fathers they abstain from such victims, they must also abstain from all animal food, in accordance with the opinions of Pythagoras, who thus showed his respect for the soul and its bodily organs. But if, as they say, they abstain that they may not eat along with *daimones*, I admire their wisdom, in having at length discovered, that whenever they eat they eat with *daimones*, although they only refuse to do so when they are looking upon a slain victim; for when they eat bread, or drink wine, or taste fruits, do they not receive these things, as well as the water they drink and the air they breathe, from certain *daimones*, to whom have been assigned these different provinces of nature? We must either not live, and indeed not come into this life at all, or we must do so on condition that we give thanks and first-fruits and prayers to *daimones*, who have been set over the things of this world: and that we must do as long as we live, that they may prove good and kind. They must make their choice between two alternatives. If they refuse to render due service to the gods, and to respect those who are set over this service, let them not come to manhood, or marry wives, or have children, or indeed take any share in the affairs of life; but let them depart hence with all speed, and leave no posterity behind them, that such a race may become extinct from the face of the earth. Or, on the other hand, if they will take wives, and bring up children, and taste of the fruits of the earth, and partake of all the blessings of life, and bear its appointed sorrows (for nature herself hath allotted sorrows to all men; for sorrows must exist, and earth is the only place for them), then must they discharge the duties of life until they are released from its bonds, and render due honour to those beings who control the affairs of this life, if they would not show themselves ungrateful to them. For it would be unjust in them, after receiving the good things which they dispense, to pay them no tribute in return.

Of course, that carried with it a profound obligation: I had to be worthy of my food. If it was paying the price to keep me alive, then damn it, I needed to make sure that that meant something, that I wasn't just sitting on my ass passing the time, merely existing as opposed to truly living. Every day I would take more and use that to do more. I'm not sure it mattered all that much to my food – their life and experiences on this mortal plane were over and would be just as over whether they ended up on my plate or stuck to the tire of a car. But it mattered to me and in the end that's all I'm responsible for. Myself. My feelings. My thoughts. My actions. In all the world, that's the only thing I could truly control – and that is made possible only through the food I eat.

It's a choice we all must make, and I don't fault anyone for how they choose. But we need to do it with our eyes open, knowing what it is we're doing and why. If nothing else, sacrifice forces us to do so, to confront all of our unexamined assumptions.

Some Background on the Toys of Dionysos

It is impossible to say when, exactly, myths of Dionysos' *sparagmós* began to circulate in ancient Greece – though judging by their wide dispersal and the archaic nature of the rites associated with them, one can safely assume that they had a fairly early origin. The myths varied in where they were located, how the deed was done, who the instigators were, the age of the god at the time it happened and their attributed meaning, but all agree that he suffered something terrible – just like the grape that is torn from the vine and crushed to make wine or the forest creature that's hunted down and rent apart by his frenzied devotees, Dionysos was killed and savagely dismembered.

One strand of this myth became attached to the Thracian shaman Orpheus and those who composed inspired verse in his famous name. However this version did not leap fully-formed from the prophetic head of Orpheus – indeed we can carefully trace its historical accretions. For instance, it was in the fifth century BCE that the name of "Titans" was first attached to Dionysos' assailants by Onomokritos, an Athenian *chresmologue* who was caught forging oracles of Mousaios and spent some time as an exile at the Persian court. (Pausanias, *Description of Greece* 8.37.5; Herodotos, *The Histories* 7.6) And mankind rising from the ash of the Titans who were blasted by Zeus' lightning-bolt – you don't get all of those threads tied together until the Neoplatonic scholar Olympiodoros in the sixth century CE, close to a thousand years later. And the only one to call the tragic child "Zagreus" was the 5th century CE poet Nonnos of Panopolis – ironic since most people, myself included until fairly recently, tend to favor this name when discussing the myth, even though its proposed derivation from *za agrios* "the Great Hunter" or from *zagre* a "pit for the capture of live animals" (Hesychios s.v.) seems an improbable *epiklesis* for an infant, divine or otherwise.

It is harder to pinpoint when the Toys of Dionysos came into the picture. Our earliest definitive reference to them is the *Gurôb Papyrus* which has been confidently dated to the third century BCE. This text, a fragmentary script for some kind of Bacchic Orphic ceremony (most likely an initiation) found in Egypt, reads:

> Accept ye my great offering as the payment for my lawless fathers.
> Save me, great Brimo ...
> and Demeter and Rhea ...
> and the armed Kouretes: let us ... and we will make fine sacrifices.
> A ram and a he-goat ... boundless gifts.
> ... and by the law of the river ...
> Taking of the goat ... let him eat the rest of the meat ...
> Let no uninitiated look on!
> Prayer of the ...
> I call on ... Eubouleus, and I call the Maenads who cry Euoi ...
> You having parched with thirst ... the friends of the feast ...
> And let us call upon the Queen of the broad Earth,
> Grant the blessings of Demeter and Pallas unto us.
> O Eubouleus, Erikepaios, save me! Phanes!
> Hurler of Lightning!
> THERE IS ONE DIONYSOS.
> Tokens ... god through the bosom.
> Having drunk ... ass cowboy ...
> Password: up and down to the ... and what has been given to you.
> Consume it, put it into the basket ...
> ... cone, bull-roarer, knucklebones, mirror.

Dating from the reign of the Makedonian pharaoh Ptolemy Philopator, the *Gurôb Papyrus* is thought to be one of the *hieroi logoi* he ordered collected and brought to the capital in his royal edict:

> Those in the country districts who impart initiation into the mysteries of Dionysos are to come down by river to Alexandria, those residing not farther than Naucratis within 10 days after the promulgation of this decree, those beyond Naucratis within 20 days, and register themselves before Aristoboulos at the registry office within 3 days of the day of their arrival, and they shall immediately declare from whom they have received the rites for three generations back and give in the Sacred Discourse sealed, each man writing upon his copy his own name. (*Berlin Papyrus* 11774, verso)

Coincidentally – or perhaps not, since scholars hypothesize that the project was undertaken in Alexandria – around this time an effort was made to collect and systematize the various Orphic pseudepigrapha that had been circulating since at least the fifth or fourth centuries BCE when members of the school of Pythagoras (the founder included) are credited with forging them. Containing cosmological, mythological, ritual poems and other texts, this work was known as *The Rhapsodies in 24 Books* and is the primary means by which Orphic lore was transmitted in late antiquity. It almost certainly contained an account of the Toys and their symbolic meaning.

Clement of Alexandria (150-215 CE) (first of the Christians to deserve the designation *philosophos*) is our next witness, and in the second book of his *Protreptikos Pros Hellenas* (or *Exhortation to the Greeks*) he expressly attributes them to a poem by Orpheus:

> The mysteries of Dionysos are wholly inhuman; for they say that the Curetes danced around his cradle clashing their weapons, and the Titans having come upon them by stealth, and having beguiled him with childish toys, these very Titans tore him limb from limb when but a child, as the bard of this mystery, the Thracian Orpheus, says:
>
>> "Kōnos and rhombos and a doll with bending limbs and beautiful golden apples from the clear-voiced Hesperides."
>
> And so it is not useless to put forth for censure the useless *symbola* of your rite: knuckle-bone, ball, top, apples, bull-roarer, mirror, wool.
>
> Athene, to resume our account, having abstracted the heart of Dionysos received the name Pallas from its palpitating (*pallein*). And the Titans who had torn him limb from limb, setting a caldron on a tripod, and throwing into it the members of Dionysos, first boiled them down, and then fixing them on spits, "held them over the fire." But Zeus having appeared, since he was a god, having speedily perceived the savour of the pieces of flesh that were being cooked,– that savour which your gods agree to have assigned to them as their perquisite, assails the Titans with his thunderbolt, and consigns the members of Dionysos to his son Apollo to be interred. And he – for he did not disobey Zeus – bore the dismembered corpse to Parnassos, and there deposited it.

Although there were a few allusions here and there in the interim, the next author to give a full account of them was Arnobius of Sicca, who left behind a promising career as a rhetorician in African Numidia to become a

Christian apologist during the contentious reign of Diocletian. His book *Adversus gentes* (*Against the Nations*) has this to say regarding the Toys:

> But those other Bacchanalia also we refuse to proclaim, in which there is revealed and taught to the initiated a secret not to be spoken; how Liber, when taken up with boyish sports, was torn asunder by the Titans; how he was cut up limb by limb by them also, and thrown into pots that he might be cooked; how Jupiter, allured by the sweet savour, rushed unbidden to the meal, and discovering what had been done, overwhelmed the revellers with his terrible thunder, and hurled them to the lowest part of Tartarus. As evidence and proof of which, the Thracian bard handed down in his poems: knuckle-bones, mirror, spinning tops, spinning wheels, and round balls, and golden apples taken from the Hesperides. (5.19)

And our final source is the Christian astrologer Iulius Firmicus Maternus, a Sicilian of Rome's senatorial class who flourished during the reigns of Constantine the Great and his successors and whose *De errore profanarum religionum* (*On the error of profane religions*) states:

> Liber was the son of Jove, a king of Crete. Considering that he was born out of wedlock, his father's attentions to him were excessive. The wife of Jove, whose name was Juno, was filled with a stepmother's anger and sought in every way by guile to bring about the death of the child. Now the father was setting out on a journey, and because he knew of the concealed displeasure of his wife, and in order to prevent her from acting treacherously in her fury, he entrusted the care of his son to guards who in his opinion were to be trusted. Juno, being thus given an opportune moment for her crime, and with fuel added to her rage through the circumstance that the father had on his departure handed over to the boy his throne and his sceptre, first of all corrupted the guardians with royal payments and gifts, then stationed her followers, called Titans, in the inner part of the palace, and with the aid of rattles and a mirror of ingenious workmanship so distracted his childish mind that he left his royal seat and was brought to the place of ambush, led there by the irrational impulse of childhood. (6)

That's it. The myth as we know it rests on four sources – three of which are hostile outsiders to the Bacchic Orphic mysteries. If they are all relying on the same single source – such as the *24 Rhapsodies* – they are doing so poorly. Not only do they disagree on essential details of the myth but their lists of Toys are all different, each author leaving out or including items which their fellows do not.

To be fair, I think that's because they weren't relying on the same single source and the Dionysian and Orphic individuals they got their information from didn't feel obligated to adhere to a canonical list in the first place.

The Toys – as reminders of Dionysos' suffering and what they themselves had gone through during initiation, as well as other symbolic associations the items were laden with – were indeed deeply important to these individuals, but since *teletai* were communicated via itinerant religious specialists or through small, autonomous groups with unique lineages, legitimacy was often gained through having an idiosyncratic – and therefore more true than one's neighbors' – interpretation of things. The ancient Greeks were just as competitive in religion as they were in all other aspects of life, remember. Most of them wouldn't know what the hell you were talking about if you read passages from Thomas Bullfinch or Edith Hamilton at them.

We know that the Toys were important from the initiates' own testimony.

Consider what Apuleius (of *Golden Ass* fame) related during his trial for ensorcelling the affections of a rich widow, proof of which was supposedly the strange tchotchkes he kept around his domicile:

> I have been initiated into various of the Greek mysteries, and preserve with the utmost care certain emblems and mementoes of my initiation with which the priests presented me. There is nothing abnormal or unheard of in this. Those of you here present who have been initiated into the mysteries of Father Liber alone, know what you keep hidden at home, safe from all profane touch and the object of your silent veneration. But I, as I have said, moved by my religious fervour and my desire to know the truth, have learned mysteries of many a kind, rites in great number, and diverse ceremonies [...] Could anyone who has any idea of religion still find it strange that a man initiated in so many divine mysteries should keep at home some tokens of recognition of the cults and should wrap them in linen cloth, the purest veil for sacred objects? For wool, the excrescence of an inert body extracted from a sheep, is already a profane garment in the prescriptions of Orpheus and Pythagoras. (*Apologia* 55-56)

The word Apuleius uses to describe these "tokens" is *crepundia* (toys or trinkets) a term we will be discussing more fully momentarily.

Much earlier the Roman *imperator* Marcus Antonius (like Ptolemy Philopator a "Neos Dionysos" or mortal incarnation of the god) had his playthings too, as Sokrates the Rhodian related in the third book of his *History of the Civil War.*

> Antony himself, when he was staying at Athens, a short time after this, prepared a very superb scaffold to spread over the theatre, covered with green wood such as is seen in the caves sacred to Dionysos; and from this scaffold he suspended drums and fawn-skins, and all the other toys which one names in connection with Dionysos, and then sat there with his friends, getting drunk from daybreak, a band of musicians, whom he had sent for from Italy, playing to him all the time, and all the Greeks around being collected to see the sight. (As quoted in Athenaios' *Deipnosophistai* 4.29)

The Toys were immensely popular in Southern Italy, appearing frequently on cups, vases and other ritual items:

> A good many Italiote choes show the same pictures as the Attic ones. Youths pouring a libation on an altar from an ornamented chous; a boy with a painted chous and an obelias-cake (reminding one of a streptos), standing near a table; a youth sitting near an altar; youth crowned with feathers or spikes holding out a garland; – all these pictures bring us into a well-known sphere. A jug-race is depicted on an Italiote chous. A boy juggling with three balls, using only one hand, surpasses the skill of the Attic ball-player; hence his conceited attitude, reminding one of a circus-acrobat. Is a rattle or a streptos-cake depicted here? Neither is unfamiliar to us. The rhombos or *inyx* is shown on many Attic vases, but not on Attic choes: it occurs on this Lucanian chous. The chthonic connection of the chous is proved by the siren approaching a sacrificial altar. The chous was used in the cult at a tomb. [...] Very remarkable is the marriage of Dionysos on an Italiote vase, where the young bridegroom is represented with short horns. No Attic vase alludes so clearly to the god, whose wedding was celebrated in the Boukoleion, the bull-stable. Some of the Italiote pictures are equivalent to the theatrical scenes on Attic choes: travesty of Herakles, seen pilfering chous and omphalos-cake from a woman at the Anthesteria; a farce of masked actors on a luxuriously decorated chous; the results of over-eating; a scene at a fair: phlyakes on a merry-go-round to the accompaniment of the flute. Other subjects are a boy hastening to the revel; a single head; women holding mirrors and birds. (Richard Hamilton, *Choes and Anthesteria* 50-51)

A funerary gold leaf from Thessalian Pherae dating from around 300 BCE bears the following inscription, attesting the eschatological import of the Toys:

> Send me to the *thiasoi* of the *mystai*: I have the ritual objects of Bakchios and the rites of Demeter Chthonia and of the Mountain Mother. (*OF* 493c)

And in a similarly Bacchic-Eleusinian syncretic milieu, several of the Toys are mentioned alongside other mystic tokens by Epiphanios:

> And how many mysteries and rites do the Greeks have? As the women who go to the *megara* and those who celebrate the Thesmophoria are different between themselves, so many other things are different: the mysteries of Deo and Pherephatta at Eleusis, and shameful actions in the sanctuaries there, nakednesses of women, to put it politely, drums and cakes, a bull-roarer and a basket, worked wool and cymbals, and *kykeon* prepared in the beaker. (*Exposition on the Faith* 10)

Nor was this the only mystery tradition that received a Bacchic Orphic infusion – Dionysos was identified with the Samothracian deities, as both Clement of Alexandria:

> If you wish to inspect the orgies of the Corybantes, then know that, having killed their third brother, they covered the head of the dead body with a purple cloth, crowned it, and carrying it on the point of a spear, buried it under the roots of Olympus. These mysteries are, in short, murders and funerals. And the priests of these rites, who are called kings of the sacred rites by those whose business it is to name them, give additional strangeness to the tragic occurrence, by forbidding parsley with the roots from being placed on the table, for they think that parsley grew from the Corybantic blood that flowed forth; just as the women, in celebrating the Thesmophoria, abstain from eating the seeds of the pomegranate which have fallen on the ground, from the idea that pomegranates sprang from the drops of the blood of Dionysos. Those Corybantes also they call Cabiric; and the ceremony itself they announce as the Cabiric mystery. For those two identical fratricides, having abstracted the box in which the phallos of Bacchus was deposited, took it to Etruria–dealers in honourable wares truly. They lived there as exiles, employing themselves in communicating the precious teaching of their superstition, and presenting phallic symbols and the box for the Tyrrhenians to worship. And some will have it, not improbably, that for this reason Dionysos was called Attis, because he was mutilated. And what is surprising at the Tyrrhenians, who were barbarians, being thus initiated into these foul indignities, when among the Athenians, and in the whole of Greece–I blush to say it– the shameful legend about Demeter holds its ground?

and the author of the *Orphic Argonautika* attest:

> Then, I sang, of the race of powerful Brimo, and the destructive acts of the Giants, who spilled their gloomy seed from the sky begetting the men of old, whence came forth mortal stock, which resides throughout the boundless world. And I sang of the service of Zeus, and of the cult of the Mother and how wandering in the mountains of Kybele she conceived the girl Persephone by the unconquerable son of Kronos, and of the renowned tearing of Kasmeilos by Herakles [the Daktyl], and of the sacred oath of Idaeus, and of the immense oak of the Korybantes, and of the wanderings of Demeter, her great sorrow for Persephone, and her lawgiving. And also I sang of the splendid gift of the Kabeiroi, and the silent oracles of Night about Lord Bacchus, and of the sea of Samothrace and of Cyprus, and of the love of Aphrodite for Adonis. And I sang of the rites of Praxidike and the mountain nights of Athela, and of the lamentations of Egypt, and of the holy offerings to Osiris.

And in their shrine at Thebes, as W. K. C. Guthrie relates, his Toys were discovered in plentiful numbers:

> Among the heaps of votive offerings found in the shrine were a number of objects, some in bronze and some in clay, which are unmistakably spinning-tops, and yet others in the form of knucklebones. Although these are the most striking examples, there are others too whose identification as playthings is scarcely more doubtful, tiny cups and jugs and glass beads. A list of dedicated objects has also come to light, and includes four knucklebones, a top and a whip. (*Orpheus and Greek Religion* page 125)

At Imbros (another holy site of the Kabeiroi) a late inscription mentions a Lord Kasmeilos in the company of five Titans (*IG* XII 8.74). Here, too, toys were found.

In fact the Toys were so important that other Bacchic myths, having nothing to do with *sparagmós*, were devised to explain their presence in cult:

> Mystis also nursed the god after her mistress's breast, watching by the side of Lyaios with sleepless eyes. The clever handmaid taught him the art that bears her name, the mystic rites of Dionysos in the night. She prepared the unsleeping worship for Lyaios, she first shook the rattle, and clanged the swinging cymbals with the resounding double bronze; she first kindled the nightdancing torch to a flame, and cried Euion to sleepless Dionysos; she first plucked

the curving growth of ivy-clusters, and tied her flowing hair with a wreath of vine; she alone entwined the thyrsos with purple ivy, and wedged on the top of the clusters an iron spike, covered with leaves that it might not scratch Bakchos. She thought of fitting plates of bronze over the naked breast, and fawnskins over the hips. She taught Dionysos to play with the mystical casket teeming with sacred things of worship, and to use them as his childish toys. She first fastened about her body a belt of braided vipers, where a serpent coiling round the belt on both sides with encircling bonds was twisted into a snaky knot. (Nonnos, *Dionysiaka* 9.111-131)

The myth of Dionysos' dismemberment could mean very different things to different people. Sometimes even the same individual could read radically divergent things into it.

For example, to Plutarch the myth was both an *aition* (explanatory tale) of cosmic plurality:

> As for the passage and distribution into waves and water, and earth, and stars, and nascent plants and animals, they hint at the actual change undergone as a rending and dismemberment, but name the god himself Dionysos or Zagreus or Nyktelios or Isodaites. Deaths too and vanishings do they construct, passages out of life and new births, all riddles and tales to match the changes mentioned. So they sing to Dionysos dithyrambic strains, charged with sufferings and a change wherein are wanderings and dismemberment. (*On the E at Delphi*)

As well as confirmation of the Pythagorean *doxai* (doctrines) of vegetarianism and *metampsychosis* (transmigration of souls):

> For Empedokles says allegorically that souls, paying the penalty for murders and the eating of flesh and cannibalism, are imprisoned in mortal bodies. However, it seems that this account is even older, for the legendary suffering of dismemberment told about Dionysos and the outrages of the Titans on him, and their punishment and their being blasted with lightning after having tasted of the blood, this is all a myth, in its hidden inner meaning, about reincarnation. For that in us which is irrational and disorderly and violent and not divine but demonic, the ancients used the name, "Titans," and the myth is about being punished and paying the penalty. (*De Esu Carnium* 1.996b-c)

Contemporary scholars have come up with a number of theories about what this myth "originally meant."

For some it was all about the "cuisine of sacrifice," to borrow a phrase from Marcel Detienne, whose *Dionysos mis à mort* (*Dionysos Slain*) explores the ancient Greeks' notions of savage and civilized forms of ritualized animal butchery, with special attention paid to the *sparagmós* of Dionysos. In the versions of the myth found in Clement and Nonnos, the crime of the Titans isn't just their murder and cannibalistic feast but how the young bovine god was prepared – first they boil the pieces of Dionysos' flesh and then roast them on skewers, which is a complete inversion of the normal procedure (first barbeque, then stew) and thus represents the triumph of barbarity over civilization. Detienne viewed the Orphics as a bunch of teetotaling vegan proto-Protestants who vehemently rejected the structures of the *polis*, most especially when they intersected with religion. Thus he saw this myth as a means of casting aspersion on the whole sacrament of animal slaughter. Despite the fact that there's scarcely any evidence to suggest that vegetarianism was a common Orphic trait and Orpheus himself is represented as participating in numerous animal sacrifices, including one that strongly resembles Nonnos' portrayal of the myth:

> The Titans cunningly smeared their round faces with disguising chalk (*titanos*), and while he contemplated his changeling countenance reflected in a mirror they crept upon him clutching an infernal knife. [Dionysos transforms into various animals] or again like a bull emitting a terrifying roar from his mouth he butted the Titans with sharp horn. And the gates of Olympos rattled in echo and finally the bold bull collapsed: the murderers each eager for his turn with the knife chopt piecemeal the bull-shaped Dionysos. (*Dionysiaka* 6.155 ff)

> And I say to you, beloved Mousaios, son of Antiophemos, he ordered me to prepare quickly for an appropriate sacrifice. And so I built an altar of excellent oak on the shore, and putting on a robe, I offered service to the gods on behalf of the men. And then I slit the throat of an enormous bull, bending back the head to the gods, cutting up the fresh meat and pouring the blood around the fire. After I laid the heart on broken cakes, I made a libation of oil and sheep's milk. I then ordered the heroes to spread round the victim, thrusting their spears and their swords furnished with handles into the victim, and into the hide and the viscera shining in my hands. And I set up in the middle a vessel containing *kykeon*, the sacred drink of water and barley, which I carefully mixed, the first nourishing offering to Demeter. Then came the blood of the bull, and salty sea-water. I ordered the crew wreathed with crowns of olive leaves. Then filling up a golden vessel with *kykeon* by my hands, I divided it by rank so that every man could have a sip of the

powerful drink. I asked Jason to order a dry pine torch to be placed beneath, and with swift motion the divine flame ascended. (*Orphic Argonautika*)

For other scholars – most notably E. R. Dodds in *The Greeks and the Irrational* and M. L. West in *The Orphic Poems* – this myth is seen as evidence of a shamanic current within early Hellenic religion, usually thought to be transmitted through contact with the Thracians or their neighbors the Scythians. Although highly critical of applying spiritual and cultural terminology that originated among Siberian and Asian populations to the Greeks, and skeptical that such things existed among the Scythians, Anna S. Kuznetsova in her study *Shamanism and the Orphic Tradition* came up with four criteria for comparison, the first two of which are directly relevant to our myth:

> 1. "Divine election" of a shaman. Still a child, the future shaman usually sees various spirits in his dreams, who try to contact or hurt him, and various animals, who aid him. This child (almost exclusively a boy) is withdrawn into himself, sleepy, non sociable, likes to walk alone in the forest, and is noted for his 'shamanistic illness' (epilepsy and hallucinations). The elder shaman chooses him and starts to introduce him into the sacred tradition. He then prepares the neophyte for initiation (Novik, 1984:197).

> 2. Initiation. This period is difficult for the neophyte in physical and psychological terms and culminates in *overcoming* of the shamanistic illness (which is in some respects different from ordinary epilepsy). 'Mastering' his shamanistic illness, the future shaman is able to *control* the epileptic attacks. Visions which the neophyte sees are usually related with scenes of dismemberment of the initiate by the underworld spirits. They torture him and then cause his rebirth so that he comes back in a new body, already possessing unique abilities. These visions were not an exclusive privilege of shamans. Smiths among Siberian peoples, for instance, practiced a similar ritual of initiation.

Which leads us to the third strain of interpretation, namely that this myth represents a primitive rite of passage – specifically a passage out of childhood.

There is a lot to commend this particular theory – for instance, an epigram by Leonidas of Tarentum commemorates Philokles' offering up the tokens of his childhood to Hermes, guide of souls, so that the god will lead him through the transition into adulthood – the beginning of a new life necessitating the death of the old:

> This loud wood rattle, this silent ball,
> Philokles gives Hermes these things.
> The bone-dice he once loved, his top,
> he renders up his childhood's toys.
> (*Greek Anthology*, 6.309)

Tokens, you will note, that perfectly mirror the Toys of Dionysos.

Toys play an important role in the rape of Kore-Persephone which is often thought to represent a similar transition from maidenhood to adult status, this time mediated through the rite of marriage. In Claudian's late treatment of the myth a distraught Ceres comes back to the tower where she has entombed her daughter and set terrifying dragons to guard her, only to discover the girl missing, her toys pathetically discarded:

> She weeps not nor bewails the ill; only kisses the loom and stifles her dumb complaints amid the threads, clasping to her bosom, as though it had been her child, the spindles her child's hand had touched, the wool she had cast aside, and all the toys scattered in maiden sport. She scans the virgin bed, the deserted couch, and the chair where Proserpine had sat: even as a herd, whose drove the unexpected fury of an African lion or bands of marauding beasts have attacked, gazes in amaze at the vacant stall, and, too late returned, wanders through the emptied pastures, sadly calling to the unreplying steers. (*De Raptu Proserpine* 3.159-169)

Toys play a different and much more direct role, however, in the *Homeric Hymn to Demeter*, where the as-yet-nameless Kore plays in a soft meadow and is attracted by a wonderfully beautiful narcissus, described as an *athurma*, "toy" (15-16) when:

> In wonder she stretched out both hands to take the beautiful toy, and the wide earth opened up beneath her.

Commenting on this passage in *The Toys of Dionysos*, Olga Levaniouk writes:

> She reaches with both hands for the flower, and her gesture is distinctly childish, almost infant-like, her attention suddenly absorbed by the "toy." For Dionysos, too, the terrifying experience comes as he is playing with beautiful, wondrous things, and the word used by Clement for the toys is *athurmata*, the very word used of Kore's narcissus in the *Homeric Hymn*.

While in this enraptured state, Kore is literally carried off, dragged to hell by its liege who is soon to become her lawfully wedded husband, their union sealed by the seeds of the pomegranate, fruit sacred to Hera and Aphrodite and the other goddesses of matrimony – an act which earns her a radiant name, Persephone.

The sacrifice of toys is found in other rites of womanhood, as another epigram from the *Greek Anthology* attests, this one honoring Timareta, a maiden (*korê*) who died before her marriage, but after she had dedicated her dolls to Artemis *Limnatis*:

> Timareta before her wedding dedicated her tambour and her lovely ball and the hair-net that held her hair. Her dolls (*korai*), too, to Artemis of the Lake, a *korê* to a *korê*, as is fitting, and the clothing of the dolls. Daughter of Leto, do you place your hand over the girl Timareta and in purity may you preserve her purity. (6.280)

Abduction lies behind the myth of Dionysos' Toys as well. You may recall that Apuleius referred to them as *crepundia*. Christopher Francese, in his book *Ancient Rome in So Many Words*, writes:

> *Crepundia* derives from the verb meaning "to rattle" (*crepare*) and refers in the first instance to the metal charms jingled to try and calm fussing babies. From there *crepundia* comes to stand in as a symbol for early childhood itself. Unlike today, when such things are generally mass-produced, a Roman tot's *crepundia* were homemade and individualized. They might be inscribed with the name of the mother or father, or include some distinctive figurines. Archaeologists have found bells, clappers, letters of ivory, children's utensils for eating and drinking, and many other objects that served this purpose.

These trinkets bear more than a passing resemblance to the Toys of Dionysos, as Harry Thurston Peck (*Harpers Dictionary of Classical Antiquities*) makes clear:

> (τὰ σπάργανα). A generic term for children's playthings, such as rattles, dolls, toy hatchets, swords, etc. The name is also given to objects of a similar description tied about the necks of children, either as amulets or for purposes of identification (Plaut. Mil. Glor. v. 6; Cist. iv. 1, 13; Rud. iv. 4; Oed. Tyr. 1035). Specimens of these are represented as worn on the neck of a child in a statue of the Museo PioClementino —viz., a half-moon (*lunula*) on the top of the right shoulder; then a double axe (*securicula ancipes*); next a bucket (*situla argenteola*); a sort of flower, not mentioned; a little sword (*ensiculus aureolus*); a little hand (*manicula*); then another half-moon; a dolphin (*delphin*), etc.

A footnote on Plaut. Rud. iv 4 reads:

> These *crepundia,* "trinkets" or "toys," seem to have been not unlike the amulets, or charms, in metal, of the present day. As kidnapping was in ancient times much more prevalent than now, these little articles, if carefully preserved by the child, might be the means of leading to the discovery of its parents; at the same time it may be justly asked how it came to pass that the kidnapper should allow such damning evidence of his villainy to remain in existence?

A good question, and one that brings us back to the myth of Dionysos' dismemberment – which may not have been committed by the ancient ancestral spirits who had been cast into Tartaros, but rather by people much closer to home. The very ones who had been put in charge of protecting him – the Kouretes, Koyrbantes or Kaberoi. Nonnos, like Clement, portrays them as guardians of the infant Dionysos:

> The goddess took care of him; and while he was yet a boy, she set him to drive a car drawn by ravening lions. Within that godwelcoming courtyard, the tripping Korybantes would surround Dionysos with their childcherishing dance, and clash their swords, and strike their shields with rebounding steel in alternate movements, to conceal the growing boyhood of Dionysos; and as the boy listened to the fostering noise of the shields he grew up under the care of the Korybantes like his father. (*Dionysiaka 9.160 ff*)

Earlier he had described their "childcherishing" dance thusly:

> Already the bird of morning was cutting the air with loud cries; already the helmeted bands of desert-haunting Korybantes were beating on their shields in the Knossian dance, and leaping with rhythmic steps, and the oxhides thudded under the blows of the iron as they whirled them about in rivalry, while the double pipe made music, and quickened the dancers with its rollicking tune in time to the bounding steps. Aye, and the trees whispered, the rocks boomed, the forests held jubilee with their intelligent movings and shakings, and the Dryades did sing. Packs of bears joined the dance, skipping and wheeling face to face; lions with a roar from emulous throats mimicked the triumphant cry of the priests of the Kabeiroi, sane in their madness; the revelling pipes rang out a tune to honour of Hekate, divine friend of dogs, those single pipes, which the horn-polisher's art invented in Kronos's days. The noisy Korybantes with their ringing din awoke Kadmos early in the morning; the Sidonian seamen also with one accord, hearing the never-silent oxhide at

dawn, rose from their rattling pebbly pallets and left the brine-beaten back of the shore. (3.61ff)

A less poetic but no less evocative account of them is provided by Strabo:

> Pherekydes says that nine Kyrbantes were sprung from Apollon and Rhetia, and that they took up their abode in Samothrake; and that three Kabeiroi and three Nymphai called Kabeirides were the children of Kabeiro, the daughter of Proteus, and Hephaistos, and that sacred rites were instituted in honor of each triad. Demetrios of Skepsis says that it is probable that the Kouretes and the Korybantes were the same, being those who had been accepted as young men, or 'youths,' for the war-dance in connection with the holy rites of the Mother of the Gods, and also as *korybantes* from the fact that they 'walked with a butting of their heads' in a dancing way. These are called by the poet *betarmones*: 'Come now, all ye that are the best *betarmones* of the Phaiakes.' And because the Korybantes are inclined to dancing and to religious frenzy, we say of those who are stirred with frenzy that they are 'korybantising.'

Several sources mention the "Titans" applying dust, chalk or ash to disguise their faces, which may have been what inspired Onomokritos to give them that name. Eustathius the Byzantine lexicographer writes:

> We apply the word *titanos* in general to dust, in particular to what is called asbestos, which is the white fluffy substance in burnt stones. It is so called from the Titans in mythology, whom Zeus in the story smote with his thunderbolts and consumed to dust. For from them, the fine dust of stones which has crumbled from excessive heat, so to speak Titanic heat, is called titanic, as though a Titanic penalty had been accomplished upon it. And the ancients call dust and gypsum *titanos*.

Thus the Korybantes became Titans by applying *titanos* to their faces. Interesting parallels to the myth of Dionysos' dismemberment are found in accounts of the rite of *enthronismos* which was found in the cults of Cybele, the Samothracian gods, the Koyrbantes, the Eleusinian mysteries and Bacchic Orphic groups. These select quotes should give you a sense of the salient features of this rite.

> They are doing just the same thing as those in the rite of the Korybantes do, when they perform the enthronement ceremony with the one who is about to be initiated. In that situation too there

is some dancing and playing around, as you know if you have been initiated. (Plato, *Euthydemos* 277d)

Socrates: Do you want to know the truth of things divine, the way they really are?
Strepsiades: Why, yes, if it's possible.
Soc: ....and to converse with the spirits in the clouds?
Strep: Without a doubt.
Soc: Then be seated on this sacred couch.
Strep: [*sitting down*]
I am seated.
Soc: Now take this chaplet.
Strep: Why a chaplet? Alas, Socrates! Would you sacrifice me like Athamas?
Soc: No, these are the rites of initiation.
Strep: And what is it I am to gain?
Soc: You'll learn to be a clever talker, to rattle off a speech, to strain your words like flour. Just keep still.
[*Socrates sprinkles flour all over Strepsiades.*]
Strep: By Zeus! That's no lie! Soon I shall be nothing but wheat-flour, if you powder me in that fashion.
Soc: Old man, be quiet. Listen to the prayer.
(Aristophanes, *Nephelai* 250-300)

On attaining manhood, you abetted your mother in her initiations and the other rituals, and read aloud from the cultic writings. At night, you mixed the libations, purified the initiates, and dressed them in fawnskins. You cleansed them off with clay and cornhusks, and raising them up from the purification, you led the chant, 'The evil I flee, the better I find.' And it was your pride that no one ever emitted that holy ululation so powerfully as yourself. I can well believe it! When you hear the stentorian tones of the orator, can you doubt that the ejaculations of the acolyte were simply magnificent? In the daylight, you led the fine *thiasos* through the streets, wearing their garlands of fennel and white poplar. You rubbed the fat-cheeked snakes and swung them above your head crying 'Euoi Saboi' and dancing to the tune of *hues attes, attes hues*. Old women hailed you 'Leader', 'mysteries instructor', 'ivy-bearer', '*liknon* carrier', and the like. (Demosthenes, *On the Crown* 259-60)

So it is just as if someone were to initiate a man, Greek or barbarian, leading him into some mystic shrine overwhelming in its size and beauty. He would see many mystic spectacles and hear many such voices; light and darkness would appear to him in alternation, and a myriad other things would happen. Still more, just as they are accustomed to do in the ritual called enthronement, the initiators, having enthroned the initiands, dance in circles around them. Is it at all likely that this man would experience nothing in his soul and that he would not suspect that what was taking place was done with a wiser understanding and preparation? ... Still more, if, not humans like the initiands, but immortal gods were initiating mortals, and night and day, both in the light and under the stars were, if it is right to speak so, literally dancing around them eternally. (Dio Chrysostom, *Oration* 12.33-34)

When the soul comes to the point of death, it suffers something like those who participate in the great initiations (*teletai*). Therefore the word *teleutan* closely resembles the word *teleisthai* just as the act of dying resembles the act of being initiated. At first there are wanderings and toilsome running about in circles and journeys through the dark over uncertain roads and culs de sacs; then, just before the end, there are all kinds of terrors, with shivering, trembling, sweating, and utter amazement. After this, a strange and wonderful light meets the wanderer; he is admitted into clean and verdant meadows, where he discerns gentle voices, and choric dances, and the majesty of holy sounds and sacred visions. Here the now fully initiated is free, and walks at liberty like a crowned and dedicated victim, joining in the revelry. (Plutarch, *De Anima* fragment preserved in Stobaios *Florigelium* 120)

This rite can be favorably compared with the Spartan Krypteia (*Life of Lycurgus*, 28, 3–7) and a similar Cretan institution described by Strabo in the 10th book of his *Geography*:

They have a peculiar custom in regard to love affairs, for they win the objects of their love, not by persuasion, but by abduction; the lover tells the friends of the boy three or four days beforehand that he is going to make the abduction; but for the friends to conceal the boy, or not to let him go forth by the appointed road, is indeed a most disgraceful thing, a confession, as it were, that the boy is unworthy to obtain such a lover; and when they meet, if the abductor is the boy's equal or superior in rank or other respects, the friends pursue him and lay hold of him, though only in a very gentle way, thus satisfying the custom; and after that they cheerfully turn the boy over to him to lead away; if, however, the abductor is unworthy, they take the boy away from him. And the pursuit does not end until the boy is taken to the "Andreium" of his abductor. They regard as a worthy object of love, not the boy who is exceptionally handsome, but the boy who is exceptionally manly and decorous. After giving the boy presents, the abductor takes him away to any place in the country he wishes; and those who were present at the abduction follow after them, and after feasting and hunting with them for two months (for it is not permitted to detain the boy for a longer time), they return to the city. The boy is released after receiving as presents a military habit, an ox, and a drinking-cup (these are the gifts required by law), and other things so numerous and costly that the friends, on account of the number of the expenses, make contributions thereto. Now the boy sacrifices the ox to Zeus and feasts those who returned with him; and then he makes known the facts about his intimacy with his lover, whether, perchance, it has pleased him or not, the law allowing him this privilege in order that, if any force was applied to him at the time of the abduction, he might be able at this feast to avenge himself and be rid of the lover. It is disgraceful for those who are handsome in appearance or descendants of illustrious ancestors to fail to obtain lovers, the presumption being that their character is responsible for such a fate. But the *parastathentes* (for thus they call those who have been abducted) receive honors; for in both the dances and the races they have the positions of highest honor, and are allowed to dress in better clothes than the rest, that is, in the habit given them by their lovers; and not then only, but even after they have grown to manhood, they wear a distinctive dress, which is intended to make known the fact that each wearer has become *kleinos*, for they call the loved one "*kleinos*" and the lover "*philetor*." So much for their customs in regard to love affairs.

In other words, the myth is the *aition* for a ritual of manhood; after the boy is abducted by men disguised as frightening monsters he undergoes a series of ordeals and should he come through them victorious he will be permitted to take up his place in a warrior or hunter society and the armed dances it performed. Precisely such a scenario is described in Euripides' *Cretans*:

> Son of the Phoenician princess, child of Tyrian Europa and great Zeus, ruler over hundred-fortressed Crete—here am I, come from the sanctity of temples roofed with cut beam of our native wood, its true joints of cypress welded together with Chalybean axe and cement from the bull. Pure has my life been since the day when I became an initiate of Idaean Zeus. Where midnight Zagreus roves, I rove; I have endured his thunder-cry; fulfilled his red and bleeding feasts; held the Great Mother's mountain flame; I am set free and named by name a Bakchos of the Mailed Priests. Having all-white

garments, I flee the birth of mortals and, not nearing the place of corpses, I guard myself against the eating of ensouled flesh. (fragment 472)

The fourth theory proposed by scholars is that instead of a primitive transitional rite (which had mostly fallen out of use by the time that we start seeing accounts of the myth), the purpose of the story was to contextualize the experiences that initiates underwent after becoming identified with the deity through ecstasy and possession. In other words, a series of ritual acts they performed triggered a feeling of union with Dionysos, strengthened by the initiate suffering vicissitudes patterned after what the god had endured. This is outright stated by Harpocration:

> Others use it in a more special sense, as for example when they speak of putting a coat of clay or pitch on those who are being initiated. In this ceremony they were mimetically enacting the myth told by some persons, in which the Titans, when they mutilated Dionysos, wore a coating of gypsum in order not to be identified. (*Lexicon* s.v. titanoi)

And strongly implied by Damascius:

> Because the first Bacchus is Dionysos, possessed by the dance and the shout, by all movements of which he is the cause according to the *Laws* (II.672a5–d4) one who has consecrated himself to Dionysos, being similar to the god, takes part in his name as well. (*Commentary on the Phaedrus* 1.171)

This *mimesis* – a concept central to the tragic arts – can be found in the funerary gold leaf from Pelinna:

> Now you have died and now you have been born, thrice blessed one, on this very day. Say to Persephone that Bakchios himself freed you. A bull you rushed to milk. Quickly, you rushed to milk. A ram you fell into milk. You have wine as your fortunate honor. And rites await you beneath the earth, just as the other blessed ones.

And the gold tablet from Thurii:

> Rejoice at the experience! This you have never before experienced. You have become divine instead of mortal. You have fallen as a kid into milk. Hail, hail, as you travel on the right, through the Holy Meadow and Groves of Persephone.

Being bathed in the milk leads to renewal and *palingenesis*, as when Medeia chopped up the nurses of Dionysos and boiled them in her cauldron so that they would be rejuvenated:

> Boiling in a bronze cauldron plants whose power she knew, obtained from diverse regions, she cooked the slain Aeson with warm herbs and restored him to his original vigor. When Father Liber noticed that Aeson's old age had been expelled by Medea's medicines, he entreated Medea to change his nurses back to the vigor of youth. Agreeing to his request, she established a pledge of eternal benefit with him by restoring his nurses to the vigor of youth by giving them same medicines that rejuvenated Aeson. (*The Second Vatican Mythographer* 137-38)

Either because it represents the Milky Way which the hero arises from as a fire-breathing star after baptism, or the fertility of a mother giving milk to her newborn young. That youthful vitality is the fuel that makes possible the transformations:

> If any one asks who narrates this, then we shall quote the well-known senarian verse of a Tarentine poet which the ancients used to sing,*"Taurus draconem genuit, et taurum draco."* ["The bull begot the dragon, and the dragon a bull."] (Arnobius of Sicca, *Adversus Nationes* 5.20)

Dionysos is a bull who regenerates himself as a snake. Always dying, always being born. Hence the epithet he bore in Naples and Campania:

> In the performance of sacred rites a mysterious rule of religion ordains that the sun shall be called Apollo when it is in the upper hemisphere, that is to say, by day, and be held to be Dionysos, or Liber Pater, when it is in the lower hemisphere, that is to say, at night. Likewise, statues of Liber Pater represent him sometimes as a child and sometimes as a young man; again, as a man with a beard and also as an old man, as for example the statue of the god which the Greeks call Bassareus and Briseus, and that which in Campania the Neapolitans worship under the name Hebon. (Macrobius, *Saturnalia* Book 1.18.7-10)

Dionysos Hebon (the Youthful) was represented as a bull with a human head – the inverse of Asterion, the Minotaur. Before Dionysos is rent apart by the Titans he becomes entranced by staring at his reflection in a mirror: according to the Starry Bull tradition what he sees is himself in the Labyrinth.

Of course there's no reason why all of these scholarly theories cannot be simultaneously true without necessarily exhausting the semantic possibility of the myth. It is all of these things and so very much more.

Sphaira the Ball

The first of Dionysos' Toys that we'll be discussing was called σφαῖρα (*sphaira*) by Clement of Alexandria and *pila* by Arnobius of Sicca – a small round ball.

In an interesting parallel with our myth, Zeus was said to have been given a ball as a distraction so that his infant cries would not attract the attention of his Titanic father Kronos who sought to destroy and devour him. According to Apollonios of Rhodes this ball was then given to Eros by the goddess Aphrodite:

> Aphrodite said, 'Will you be good and do me a favour I am going to ask of you? Then I will give you one of Zeus' lovely toys, the one that his fond nurse Adrasteia made for him in the Idaian cave when he was still a child and liked to play. It is a perfect ball; Hephaistos himself could not make you a better toy. It is made of golden hoops laced together all the way round with double stitching; but the seams are hidden by a winding blue band. When you throw it up, it will leave a fiery trail behind it like a meteor in the sky.'
> (*Argonautica* 3. 132 ff)

The ball was a common attribute of the childish love-god, used by him to initiate affairs:

> Eros with the golden curls
> throws me the purple ball
> and calls me to play with
> the girl with the bright-colored sandals.
> (Anakreon, fragment 5)

In Southern Italy this act was given eschatological significance:

> A happy and unique find is a krater in the Naples museum, because the painting is clarified by an inscription. A winged youth throws a colorful embroidered ball to a hesitant woman. Looking outward but at the same time inward, she is resting one hand on a stele which bears the inscription. The stele is a *horos*, a boundary stone, and here it probably marks the boundary of the hesitant woman's home country, which she, wearing no ornament and lightly clad, must now leave. She does not reach for the ball, but looks with the shadow of a sly smile at the messenger who has thrown it to her. She *will* go. On the other side stands a woman with a grave expectant face, holding out to her a mirror and a *tainia*, a festive ribbon. The woman who thus hesitates is not a *hetaera*; she is a bride-to-be, but one who already knows. She would prefer not to travel this road. It is Eros — golden-curled in Anakreon, here darkhaired — who summons the girl to the game of love with his ball. The ball is an erotic message. Whence and whither? Eros is the only intermediary. What the hesitant woman thinks we are told by the inscription on the boundary stone: "They have thrown me the ball" — "they" in the plural, not any definite individual, even if the bridegroom is waiting in the background. The plural does not befit the language of ancient erotic poetry, but it does that of sepulchral epigrams: "The goddesses of fate ... led me down to Hades." Ordinarily they are sent a messenger to act as a guide, in this case, Eros. Often it was Hermes, the guide of souls. The woman to whom the *daimon* of love has been sent as messenger and guide still hesitates to accept death fully, though it has already taken possession of her. She is unwilling, but she goes nevertheless to the great erotic adventure. For such *was* death in the atmosphere of the Anthesteria. Eros with the ball is an aspect of death. (Carl Kerényi, *Dionysos Archetypal Image of Indestructible Life* 365-66)

While in Sparta, the ball represented a different transition – young men who were leaving behind their ephebehood were called *sphaireis* (Böckh, *Corp. Inscr.* n1386, 1432.) This name became attached to them because of the popularity of ball-play in the *gymnasion* which often had a whole room (called a *sphairistra*) set aside for it, and in some places even an instructor (*sphairistrikós*) who specialized in teaching the young men skillful mastery of the ball.

One can see why these sports played such an important role in the exercise and training of youths from Athenaios' account:

> Great are the exertion and fatigue attendant upon contests of ball-playing, and violent twisting and turning of the neck. Hence Antiphanes: "Damn me, what a pain I've got in my neck!" He describes the game of *phaininda* thus: "He seized the ball and passed it with a laugh to one, while the other player he dodged; from one he pushed it out of the way, while he raised another player to his feet amid resounding shouts of 'out of bounds,' 'too far,' 'right beside him,' 'over his head,' 'on the ground,' 'up in the air,' 'too short,' 'pass it back in the scrimmage.'" The game was called *phaininda* either from the players shooting the ball or because, according to Juba the Mauretanian, its inventor was the trainer Phainestios. Ball-players also paid attention to graceful movement. Damoxenos, at any rate, says: "What rhythm! What modesty of manner! What skill!" (*Deiponosophistai* 1.15a-c)

Ballgames were found as far back as Homer – Nausicaä (whom Agallis the Corcyraean credited with their invention) was playing at ball with her maidens when Odysseus first saw her in the land of the god-like Phaiacians (*Odyssey* 4.100), while a ball-dance was performed for Odysseus' entertainment at the court of King Alkinoos:

> Then Alkinoos told Laodamas and Halios to dance alone, for there was no one to compete with them. So they took a red ball which Polybos had made for them, and one of them bent himself backwards and threw it up towards the clouds, while the other jumped from off the ground and caught it with ease before it came down again. When they had done throwing the ball straight up into the air they began to dance, and at the same time kept on throwing it backwards and forwards to one another, while all the young men in the ring applauded and made a great stamping with their feet. Then Odysseus said: "King Alkinoos, you said your people were the nimblest dancers in the world, and indeed they have proved themselves to be so. I was astonished as I saw them." (ibid 8.370-384)

According to Herodotos, the Greeks learned *paideia* (games) from the Lydians who invented them as a distraction in a time of famine:

> The games now in use among the Greeks were invented by the Lydians at the time when they colonized Tyrrhenia. They relate that during the reign of Atys son of Manes there was a great scarcity of food in all Lydia. The Lydians bore this adversity with as much patience as they could, but when the famine did not abate they looked for remedies, and different plans were devised by different

men. Then it was that they invented the games of dice and knucklebones and ball and all other forms of game. Then, using their discovery to lighten the famine, every other day they would play for the whole day, so that they would not have to look for food, and the next day they quit their play and ate. (*The Histories* 1.94.2-4)

Getting back into the realm of Dionysos, Ioannes Laurentios Lydos interpreted the balls of the Bacchic *mystai* as symbolic of a spherical Gaia revolving around Helios, whom he syncretized with the god through clever wordplay:

> Dionysos, "because of whom is the race-post" (*di' hon hê nyssa*) – that is, the turning-post – and the cycles of time, had mysteries conducted in honor of him in secret because the Sun's shared association with the nature of the universe is hidden from everyone. And in his sacred rites they would carry along phalloi, as being the organs of generation, and a mirror, as representing the radiantly translucent heavens, and a ball, as representing the Earth. For Plato says in his *Timaios*, "to Earth, the spherical form." (*de Mensibus* 51)

There is an elegance to that image, for it calls to mind the appearance of Dionysos on the so-called *Lenäenvasen*, which Arthur Pickard-Cambridge describes as follows:

> ... in the form of a bearded mask set upon a pole, pillar, or column, often apparently of wood; the 'pillar' is usually clothed, with varying degrees of decoration; the mask of the god and the 'pillar' are often crowned with ivy to which (or to some other part of his decoration) are attached, in a number of vases, thin ritual cakes of the type known as πλακουντες, and the adornment sometimes includes grapes. The ritual is performed invariably by women, in various stages of ecstasy, with thyrsi, torches, flutes and tympana. (*The Dramatic Festivals of Athens* pp. 30-31)

This Dionysos is dark and still and somber, the quiet amid the storm, the masked pillar around which those filled with his frenzy dance and shout in ecstatic celebration. He is not completely immobile – his movements are just slow like the shoots of a plant triumphantly rising up through the soil, like the gradual formation of stalactites in a cave, like the procession of the stars through the heavens. The face of this Dionysos is always concealed in shadows, except for his eyes which are bright with the flames of madness and gaze into the depths of your soul and beyond. His voice echoes across a vast chasm even when he is nearer to you than your next heartbeat. There is an impenetrable denseness to his spirit, a gloom so black and so full of painful memories that even he has difficulty bearing its weight. He is ancient beyond all reckoning and yet remains unwearied by all that he has witnessed and experienced. His heart is fierce with love for the fragile and ephemeral things of this world, rejoicing and suffering along with them. He cannot turn his face away from them – he must witness it all, even if it makes him mad. And though part of him remains forever down in the caverns deep beneath the earth, another part extends upwards into our world, surrounded by an innumerable host. The lusty satyrs, the madwomen, the nymphs who nurse him and the dead who belong to him, an invisible troop of wild spirits that march unseen but clearly heard in his processions, who race through the fields and forests and city streets on certain especially dark nights in pursuit of the victims of the hunt.

This is the Dionysos I associate with the ball. And a large part of the reason why is because of the Kerényi passage I quoted earlier, which continues:

> Bearing another instrument characteristic of Dionysian dancing girls, a large *tympanon*, she is shown following the winged Eros in the passionate representation on an Apulian amphora in Bonn. It is on the basis of this painting that an erotic Dionysian abduction was for the first time recognized to be a journey to death. With the gesture of his left hand, Eros is drawing her after him – and the resisting gesture on her right hand is unmistakable.
>
> A bride such as this one with the tense, frightened face, followed by the escorting boy with a wreath – the wreath of Ariadne! – is not being led to an ordinary wedding. With this escort and this expressive face she can only be going to a mystery. With his right hand the winged Eros beckons to those who have remained far behind; it is a gesture of farewell, farewell to the *thiasos*. In the vase paintings of the south Italian group from which all the examples cited here are taken, we can also discern the details of the exodus in which only a few persons participate, the executants of a particular ceremony separate from the general *thiasos* in the open. The two possibilities presented by this ceremony – "earthly love" with a mortal silenus and "heavenly love" with the god – are indicated in an exemplary manner by a work of the Meidias painter.
>
> People do not go to "heavenly nuptials" hand in hand. To a divine encounter one is called, seduced by a superior power. Where a living person is concerned, this person will achieve the *telos* in a mystery ceremony through the *gamos*. Just this happens in the death of young people. Dionysos lured them and also summoned them with a bell; he is shown thus luring a woman on a krater in Ruvo. She follows him with the *tympanon* which will accompany her dance

when she sues for the god's love. Her face expresses the magic spell that has come over her. One of the two sileni, representing the servants who accompany her, bears both torch and *situla*. On a bell krater in Lecce a youth, naked except for the cloak thrown lightly over his shoulders, is standing before a seated woman; she is the divine maenad from whom he desires fulfillment. He has arrived as though from a journey, and the egg he brings her is the egg that is buried with the dead. She is awaiting him with a large *thyrsos*; a silenus holds another behind her. He also holds a wreath in preparation for the marriage which is to resemble that of Dionysos to Ariadne.

Throughout southern Italy the name "Ariadne" suggests itself for Dionysos' divine partner, into whom the female deceased are transformed, while the males are transformed into Dionysos. On a large bowl in Ruvo she is borne heavenward by two winged Erotes.

The youth already bears a branching, flowering *thyrsos*, but the mystery of his transformation into a true Dionysos is still to come. In another painting a maenad lures and leads a youth who is already fully equipped as a young Dionysos. On a krater in Barletta he holds not only the *thyrsos* but a kantharos in the manner of a Heros Dionysos; on a krater in Bari he holds a cluster of grapes. On a large bowl similar to that showing the erotic ascension of an Ariadne, the ways of initiation of both a man and a woman are indicated. On one side the woman, already holding the *tympanon*, is being lured by a torch-bearing Eros and a maenad. On the other side, the youth is sitting beside his tomb as heroified dead sit beside their monuments in vase paintings. Behind the tombstone – it is at the same time a boundary stone, as always in this type of representation – stands the luring maenad with a *tympanon*; behind her stands an already initiated youth bearing clusters of grapes. Both sexes achieve the same Dionysian apotheosis in death.

The pairing of Ariadne and balls is the clue of this Toy's meaning. Clue, after all, means ball:

> Clue (n.) 1590s, spelling variant of *clew* "a ball of thread or yarn," in this sense with reference to the one Theseus used as a guide out of the Labyrinth. The purely figurative sense of "that which points the way" is from 1620s. As something which a bewildered person does not have, by 1948. (*Online Etymology Dictionary*)

And Ariadne is the one who dispenses clues:

The door of the labyrinth, so difficult, which none of those before could find again, by Ariadne's aid was found by Theseus, the thread that traced the way rewound. Then Aegides, seizing Minois, spread his sails for Naxos, where, upon the shore, that cruel prince abandoned her and she, desolate in her grief and anger, found comfort in Liber's arms. He took her crown and set it in the heavens to win her there a star's eternal glory. (Ovid, *Metamorphoses* 8. 173 ff)

Astragaloi the Dice

The next of Dionysos' Toys are *astragaloi* (αστραγαλοι), dice most commonly made from the knucklebones of goats or sheep – though models have also been found carved from ivory, bronze, silver, gold marble, wood, glass and terracotta.

These bones have four sides, two of which are narrow and two broad. Each side was given a name and numerical value by the ancient Greeks, as Kostas Dervenis explains:

> The broad convex side is called *pranes*, while the broad concave side is called *hyption*. The convex narrow side is called *chion*, while the concave narrow side is called *koon*. The *koon* throw is worth six points, while the *chion* throw is worth one. Of the two broad sides, the *hyption* throw receives three points, while the *pranes* four. The *chion* throw was also called *monos* (single), and the *koon* throw *exetis* (sixes), based on the numerical values they represented. (*Oracle Bones Divination* pg. 27)

Sophokles claimed that Palamedes (who rivaled Odysseus in cunning) first invented gaming with *astragaloi* during the Trojan War. The ancients played a number of different games with *astragaloi*, but the commonest involved tossing four of them and when they landed determining their value by counting the sides facing up. If all four *astragaloi* had different sides up the throw was called Aphrodite and the player won the game; all ones was called the Dog and considered the worst throw. Though generally a children's and women's game, the Roman Emperor Octavian didn't let that dull his enthusiasm – Suetonius records his habit of gambling over *astragaloi* throws with friends during holidays such as Saturnalia and Quinquatria (*Life of Augustus* 71). Another popular version of the game (called *pentalitha* or "five stone" by Julius Pollux) resembled our jacks, with one *astragalos* being tossed in the air while the player tried to pick as many knucklebones off the floor as they could with one hand before it landed. This game is still popular in many parts of Greece, Italy and Turkey today.

Their use in divination, however, goes much further back. Plato in the *Phaidros* credits the Egyptian god Thoth, whom he equates with Hermes, with turning them into a divination system.

Divinatory *astragaloi* were found in the Neolithic village of Çatal Höyuk in Anatolia dating to the sixth millennium BCE; nearby at Izmir (the ancient Metropolis) archaeologists have unearthed a large cache of *astragaloi* from the temple of the oracular goddess Meter Gallesia, demonstrating a continuity of practice through the Hellenistic era.

In mainland Greece a similar trove of *astragaloi* was found in the Korykian Cave whose nymphs, in the form of bees, taught Hermes the art of divination as part of a bargain he struck with Apollon for his tortoise-shell lyre:

> But I will tell you another thing, son of all-glorious Maia and Zeus who holds the aegis, luck-bringing daimon of the gods. There are certain holy ones, sisters born – three virgins gifted with wings: their heads are besprinkled with white meal, and they dwell under a ridge of Parnassos. These are teachers of divination apart from me, the art which I practised while yet a boy following herds, though my father paid no heed to it. From their home they fly now here, now there, feeding on honey-comb and bringing all things to pass. And when they are inspired through eating yellow honey, they are willing to speak truth; but if they be deprived of the gods' sweet food, then they speak falsely, as they swarm in and out together. These, then, I give you; enquire of them strictly and delight your heart: and if you should teach any mortal so to do, often will he hear your response – if he have good fortune. Take these, Son of Maia, and tend the wild roving, horned oxen and horses and patient mules. (*Homeric Hymn to Hermes* 4.550-567)

These nymphs were said by Aischylos in the *Eumenides* to revel with Dionysos on the slopes of Parnassos, and they were also involved in the story of Thyia, the first woman to become a priestess of Dionysos and the prototype of the Thyiades who journeyed from Athens to perform torch-lit dances on Parnassos during winter (Pausanias, *Description of Greece* 10.6.1). A connection between dancing and *astragaloi* is also found in the *Orphic Hymn to Nature*, where Physis is described as Αψοφον αστραγαλοισι ποδων ιχνος ειλισσουσα "turning round silent traces with the ankle-bones of her feet."

Herakles, too, possessed an oracular cave which utilized *astragaloi*:

> On descending from Boura towards the sea you come to a river called Bouraikos, and to a small Herakles in a cave. He too is surnamed Bouraikos, and here one can divine by means of a tablet and dice. He who inquires of the god offers up a prayer in front of the image, and after the prayer he takes four dice, a plentiful supply of which are placed by Herakles, and throws them upon the table. For every configuration made by the dice there is an explanation expressly written on the tablet. (Pausanias, *Description of Greece* 7.25.10)

Temples, caves and oracular shrines were not the only places where *astragaloi* have turned up:

> In addition, in many children's graves archaeologists have found a sack of *astragali* in the left hand of the remains, testament not only of the parents' love for their child and of their desire to send his favorite toys with him on to the next life, but also of the inviolability of *astragali* in general and their origin in primal sacrament. (Kostas Dervenis, pg 22)

There was a strong association between *astragaloi* and childhood, according to Bekircan Tahberer:

> It is *astragaloi* that seem to characterize children in contrast to adult males. As a cynical proverb attributed to a number of political leaders put it, 'You fool children with *astragaloi* but men with oaths.' (*Astragaloi on Ancient Coins: Game Pieces or Agents of Prophecy?*)

According to an epigram by Asklepiodotos Takitos, children were awarded *astragaloi* upon reaching school age, marking one of the most important steps in their young lives.

Later when they passed out of childhood they would offer those *astragaloi* to Hermes, guide of souls, so that the god would lead them through the transition into adulthood – the beginning of a new life necessitating the death of the old:

> This loud wood rattle, this silent ball,
> Philokles gives Hermes these things.
> The bone-dice he once loved, his top,
> he renders up his childhood's toys.
> (Leonidas of Tarentum, *Greek Anthology*, 6.309)

Herodotos felt *astragaloi* had something to do with a *rite de passage* he observed during his travels through Egypt:

> They said that later this king went down alive to what the Greeks call Haides and there played dice with Demeter, and after winning some and losing some, came back with a gift from her of a piece golden cloth. From the descent of Rhampsinitos, when he came back, they said that the Egyptians celebrate a festival, which I know that they celebrate to this day, but whether this is why they celebrate, I cannot say. On the day of the festival, the priests weave a cloth and bind it as a headband on the eyes of one of their number, whom they then lead, wearing the cloth, into a road that goes to the temple of Demeter; they themselves go back, but this priest with his eyes bandaged is guided (they say) by two wolves to Demeter's temple, a distance of three miles from the city, and led back again from the temple by the wolves to the same place. These Egyptian stories are for the benefit of whoever believes such tales: my rule in this history is that I record what is said by all as I have heard it. The Egyptians say that Demeter and Dionysos are the rulers of the lower world. The Egyptians were the first who maintained the following doctrine, too, that the human soul is immortal, and at the death of the body enters into some other living thing then coming to birth; and after passing through all creatures of land, sea, and air, it enters once more into a human body at birth, a cycle which it completes in three thousand years. (*The Histories*, 2.122.1-123.2)

Which may have something to do with the Bacchic Orphic gold lamellae, where we find the animals from whom *astragaloi* were most commonly harvested associated with *palingenesis* or rebirth at Pelinna:

> Now you have died and now you have been born, thrice blessed one, on this very day. Say to Persephone that Bakchios himself freed you. A bull you rushed to milk. Quickly, you rushed to milk. A ram you fell into milk. You have wine as your fortunate honor. And rites await you beneath the earth, just as the other blessed ones.

And Thurii:

> Rejoice at the experience! This you have never before experienced. You have become divine instead of mortal. You have fallen as a kid into milk. Hail, hail, as you travel on the right, through the Holy Meadow and Groves of Persephone.

Sheep were drowned in offering to Dionysos during the *Anabasis* (Ascent) portion of his mysteries at Lerna:

> They call Dionysos up out of the water by the sound of trumpets, at the same time casting into the depths a lamb as an offering to the Keeper of the Gate. (Plutarch, *On Isis and Osiris* 364f)

Which was preceded by the *Katabasis* (Descent) to retrieve his mother, lightning-struck Semele:

> At this mountain begins the grove which consists chiefly of plane trees, and reaches down to the sea. Its boundaries are, on the one side the river Pantinos, on the other side another river, called Amymane, after the daughter of Danaus. Within the grove are images of Demeter Prosymne and of Dionysos. Of Demeter there is a seated image of no great size. Both are of stone, but in another temple is a seated wooden image of Dionysos Saotes (Savior), while by the sea is a stone image of Aphrodite. They say that the daughters of Danaus dedicated it, while Danaus himself made the sanctuary of Athena by the Pontinos. The mysteries of the Lernaeans were established, they say, by Philammon. Now the words which accompany the ritual are evidently of no antiquity and the inscription also, which I have heard is written on the heart made of *orichalcum*, was shown not to be Philammon's by Arriphon. I saw also what is called the Spring of Amphiaraus and the Alcyonian Lake, through which the Argives say Dionysos went down to Hell to bring up Semele, adding that the descent here was shown him by Palymnos. There is no limit to the depth of the Alcyonian Lake, and I know of nobody who by any contrivance has been able to reach the bottom of it since not even Nero, who had ropes made several stades long and fastened them together, tying lead to them, and omitting nothing that might help his experiment, was able to discover any limit to its depth. This, too, I heard. The water of the lake is, to all appearance, calm and quiet but, although it is such to look at, every swimmer who ventures to cross it is dragged down, sucked into the depths, and swept away. The circumference of the lake is not great, being about one-third of a stade. Upon its banks grow grass and rushes. The nocturnal rites performed every year in honor of Dionysos I must not divulge to the world at large. (Pausanias 2.37.1-3; 2.37.5-6)

While goats were sacrificed by the Ausonians in tragic rites, according to Vergil:

And they're the why, such transgressions, a goat is sacrificed
on every altar to the wine god – since our elders started to stage plays
and the sons of Theseus rewarded talent along the highways and
byeways and, with drink taken, took to hopping here and there,
a dance on greasy hides, and toppling in soft grass.
So too, Ausonian settlers – who came from Troy –
recited their rough-hewn verse to entertain the masses,
and put on scary masks cut out of bark
and called on you, Bacchus, in rousing song,
and in your honour dangled from the tips of pines tender tokens.
And it ensues that every vineyard crests and fills,
valleys teem, and deep ravines –
anywhere the god took in with his goodly gaze.
Therefore, as is only right, we accord to Bacchus due respect
with songs our fathers sang and trays of baked offerings
and, led by the horn, the sacrifical puck is set before the altar
and his spewling innards roasted on hazel skewers.
(*Georgics* 2.380-396)

Just as the Athenians did the drunken dance on oiled goat-skins (*askoliasmos*) for the hero Ikarios (whom Hyginus conflates with Ikaros, the son of Daidalos):

> *The constellation Bootes.* The Bear Watcher. Some have said that he is Icarus, father of Erigone, to whom, on account of his justice and piety, Father Liber gave wine, the vine, and the grape, so that he could show men how to plant the vine, what would grow from it, and how to use what was produced. When he had planted the vine, and by careful tending with a pruning-knife had made it flourish, a goat is said to have broken into the vineyard, and nibbled the tenderest leaves he saw there. Icarus, angered by this, took him and killed him and from his skin made a sack, and blowing it up, bound it tight, and cast it among his friends, directing them to dance around it. And so Eratosthenes says: 'Around the goat of Ikarios they first danced.' Others say that Icarus, when he had received the wine from Father Liber, straightway put full wineskins on a wagon. For this he was called Boötes. (*Astronomica* 2.2)

When one hears of bones and Dionysos, one naturally thinks of the Bacchic Orphic bone tablets found at Olbia on the Black Sea. These enigmatic phrases, representing the full paradoxical nature of Dionysos, were likely inscribed on bone because it is the body's memory, that part which survives even the funerary flame of the pyre:

SEG 28.661:
Διόνυσος. ἀλήθεια. σῶμα. ψυχή
Dionysos. Truth. Body. Soul.

SEG 28.660:
εἰρήνη. πόλεμος. ἀλήθεια. ψεῦδος. Διόνυσος
Peace. War. Truth. Lie. Dionysos

SEG 28.659:
βίος. θάνατος. βίος. ἀλήθεια. Ζαγρεύς. Διόνυσος
Life. Death. Life. Truth. Zagreus. Dionysos.

This last one, which some take as an indication of Orphic belief in *metempsychosis* or the transmigration of souls, may also be representing the process of initiation: life leading into death leading into a new type of life, one patterned after the experience of Dionysos. The word translated "truth" in this sequence – ἀλήθεια – literally means a "loss of forgetfulness."

And when one hears of knucklebones one naturally thinks of the foot or hoof, from which they were extracted. This is, after the phallos, the most quintessential Dionysian appendage, according to Marcel Detienne's *Dionysos à ciel ouvert*:

> In the world of bipeds nothing could be more banal than a fall, except perhaps when it occurs in the vicinity of Dionysos. In fact there is much evidence to suggest that the foot or leg is a key part of the Dionysiac body. Consider first Euripides' Bacchante, canonical in her happiness: regaling with evoes the god of the evoe, she leaps like a young mare, "she springs forward with a quick thrust of the leg." Symmetrically, the tragic maenad Agave returns from Kithairon with "a bacchic step", drunk with a murderous fury inspired in her by Dionysos and carrying Pentheus' bloody mask. The bacchic step, the quick forward thrust of the foot, was taught to choruses of satyrs in Athens around 500 B.C. by the dancing master Pratinas, when he paid homage to Dionysos for an art threatened by boisterous imitators: "Prince crowned with ivy, note the movement of the right foot, its kick." And when the god, wearing the mask of the foreigner, presides over the dressing of Pentheus in front of the palace of Kadmos, he shows him how a bacchant must raise his right leg at the same time as he raises the thyrsus in his right hand. This is the first of the Dionysiac gestures. More than once the god himself is invoked by his foot, as in *Antigone*, when his purifying assistance is requested so urgently to deal with the magnitude of the defilement. And then, too, Dionysos is quite simply the god who

jumps, who leaps (*pedan*) among the torches on the rocks of Delphi. He capers like a goat among the Bacchae of the night. In leaping Dionysos the foot (*pous*) encounters the verb to leap (*pedan*) and its form "to jump away from" (*ekpedan*) which is a technical term of the Dionysiac trance, referring to the moment when the leaping force invades the body and takes control of it, carrying it irresistibly along. Aristoxenus, the musicologist from Tarento, has left a clinical description from southern Italy, between Locri and Reggio. The women were taken out of themselves: *ekstaseis*. Seated and busy eating, they thought they heard a voice, a call from afar, whereupon they jumped up (*ekpedan*), and no one was able to restrain them. They then began running away from the city. To cure this epidemic evil Apollo recommended paeans, purifying chants, and spring songs, administered in a sixty-day course of treatment. Musically the result was a swelling of the ranks of composers. There is no room for doubt. The Dionysiac trance began with the foot, with leaping – and in the Dionysiac world the ability to leap was the foot's most important characteristic. All who took part in the Dionysiac feasts, or, more precisely, in rural Dionysia, were familiar with a game that involved "walking" on one leg, that is, hopping. The game was known as *askoliasmos*. (pgs 46-47)

Trochos the Wheel

Arnobius of Sicca described our next Toy as *volubiles rotulas* a "spinning wheel" which is equivalent to the Greek τροχός, κρίκος and κυκλός, words meaning "wheel," "hoop" and "circle."

From the fifth century BCE Ganymede is recognizable on pottery by his hoop and the stick he uses to drive it along; in time the stick was transformed into an ἐλατήρ (elater) or *clavis* "key" consisting of a metal hook, often shaped like its namesake, and a wooden handle.

The *trochós* was normally a bronze ring, though poorer children would make use of whatever was at hand, as Martial warns:

> Guard well your wooden cart wheel, or it will become a hoop to children, a most useful present. (*Epigrams* 14.CLXVIII)

And it was, for it exercised the whole body and taught them balance, dexterity and hand-eye coordination, for which reason the *trochós* passed into the repertoire of the *gymnasion*. In particular Hippokrates recommended its use for those with weak constitutions. A 2nd century CE medical text by Antyllos, preserved in an anthology of Oribasios, Emperor Julian's physician, describes hoop rolling as a form of physical and mental therapy. According to Harold Arthur Harris, Antyllos "indicates that at first the player should roll the hoop maintaining an upright posture, but after warming up he can begin to jump and run through the hoop. Such exercises, he holds, are best done before a meal or a bath, as with any physical exercise" (*Sport in Greece and Rome* pg 133).

The hoop was highly esteemed among the Romans, as the *Distichs* of Cato show:

> *Trocho lude; aleam fuge.* ("Play with the hoop; flee the dice.")

Although the Romans maintained the name (often calling it *Graecus trochus*) they made a few modifications after adopting it, such as fitting their hoops with metal rings that slid freely along the rim as it rolled, done according to Martial, so that the tinkling of the rings would warn passers-by of the hoop's approach (14. CLXIX).

More significantly, the *trochós* became associated with war-games and preparation for military service. Roman boys would roll the hoop and then try to throw sticks or spears through it, on which account Horace praised it as the "most manly of sports." Ovid in his *Tristia* is more specific, putting the hoop game in the same category with horsemanship, javelin-throwing and weapons practice.

This would be reason enough for Arnobius to include it among the Toys of the divine innocent, but the *trochós* and *kuklos* had a complex web of associations within Bacchic and Orphic circles and it is to these that we must look for its fuller meaning.

In some accounts Dionysos is the inventor of agriculture, first to make the wheel and wagon and yoke oxen for ploughing:

> For according to them there was born of Zeus and Persephone a Dionysos who is called by some Sabazios and whose birth and sacrifices and honours are celebrated at night and in secret, because of the disgraceful conduct which is a consequence of the gatherings. They state also that he excelled in sagacity and was the first to attempt the yoking of oxen and by their aid to effect the sowing of the seed, this being the reason why they also represent him as wearing a horn. (Diodoros Sikeliotes, *Library of History* 4.4.1)

This wagon of Dionysos shows up in his encounter with Ikarios:

> When Father Liber went out to visit men in order to demonstrate the sweetness and pleasantness of his fruit, he came to the generous hospitality of Icarius and Erigone. To them he gave a skin full of wine as a gift and bade them spread the use of it in all the other lands. Loading a wagon, Icarius with his daughter Erigone and a dog Maera came to shepherds in the land of Attica, and showed them the kind of sweetness wine had. The shepherds, made drunk by drinking immoderately, collapsed, and thinking that Icarius had given them some bad medicine, killed him with clubs. (Hyginus, *Fabulae* 130)

And also Midas, to whom he gave the golden touch and the wagon to carry his treasures:

> At the time when Father Liber was leading his army into India, Silenus wandered away; Midas entertained him generously, and gave him a guide to conduct him to Liber's company. Because of this favour, Father Liber gave Midas the privilege of asking him for whatever he wanted. Midas asked that whatever he touched should become gold. When he had been granted the wish, and came to his palace, whatever he touched became gold. When now he was being tortured with hunger, he begged Liber to take away the splendid gift. Liber bade him bathe in the River Pactolus, and when his body touched the water it became a golden colour. The river in Lydia is now called Chrysorrhoas (Golden-Flow). (*Hyginus, Fabulae 191*)

> *Kathamma lueis*. A proverb in reference to those attempting to undo something which is hard to undo. From the wagon of Midas. For an oracle had been issued to the Phrygians which said that if anyone could untie the binding of the wagon which Midas used to carry his wealth, this man would rule Asia. Alexander the Great undid it. (*Suidas s.v. Kathamma lueis*)

The wagon likewise can be found in festivals celebrating the triumph of Dionysos, such as the Dionysia:

> It is commanded to those bringing back the victory spoils that they revile and make jokes about the most famous men along with their generals, like those escorts on wagons during the Athenian festival who used to carry on with jokes but now sing improvisational poems. (Dionysios Halikarnassos, *Roman Antiquities* 7.72.11)

The Anthesteria:

> This is about those mocking openly. For in Athens at the festival of the Choes those reveling on the wagons mocked and reviled those they met and they did the same also at the Lenaia. (Photius s.v. *that from the wagons*)

And the Ptolemaeia:

> After these came a four-wheeled wagon, twenty-one feet long and twelve feet wide, drawn by one-hundred and eighty men; in this stood a statue of Dionysos, fifteen feet tall, pouring a libation from a gold goblet, and wearing a purple tunic extending to the feet, over which was a transparent saffron coat; but round his shoulders was thrown a purple mantle spangled with gold. In front of him lay a gold Laconian mixing-bowl holding one hundred and fifty gallons;

also a gold tripod, on which lay a gold censer and two saucers of gold full of cassia and saffron. Over him stretched a canopy decorated with ivy, grape-vine, and the other cultivated fruits, and hanging to it also were wreaths, ribbons, Bacchic wands, tambourines, fillets, and satyric, comic, and tragic masks. (excerpt from Kalleixenos of Rhodes in Athenaios' *Deipnosophistai* 5.196-203)

Wagons are even found on the Shield of Dionysos in Nonnos, in the section portraying the constellations:

> Beside the socket of the axle were the poles of the two heavenly Wagons, never touched by the water; for these both move head to loin together round a point higher than Okeanos, and the head of the sinking Bear always bends down exactly as much as the neck of the rising Bear stretches up. Between the two Wagons he made the Serpent, which is close by and joins the two separated bodies, bending his heavenly belly in spiral shape and turning to and fro his speckled body, like the spirals of Maiandros and its curving murmuring waters, as it runs to and fro in twists and turns over the ground. (*Dionysiaka* 25.380 ff)

In our masterful poet the turning of the Wagon's wheel gives rise to imagery of twisting, coiling serpents, spiraling, interlocked patterns and the winding course of a river famed for its meandering, which call to mind the often confusing paths our life may take.

Indeed, as Plato quotes Herakleitos as saying, "everything changes and nothing remains still" so that "you cannot step twice into the same stream" (*Kratylos* 401d). Suggestively Plato uses πάντα χωρεῖ (everything is dance-like) instead of the more commonly attested πάντα ῥεῖ (everything flows), which naturally makes one think of the circle dances of the goddess Ariadne:

> Behold the troup of dancers, like the chorus which Daidalos is said to have invented for Ariadne, daughter of Minos; young men and maidens with hands clasped and going about in a circle. (Philostratos the Younger, *Imagines* 10)

> On his voyage from Crete, Theseus put in at Delos, and having sacrificed to the god and dedicated in his temple the image of Aphrodite which he had received from Ariadne, he danced with his youths a dance which they say is still performed by the Delians, being an imitation of the circling passages in the Labyrinth, and consisting of certain rhythmic involutions and evolutions. This kind of dance, as Dikaiarchos tells us, is called by the Delians The Crane, and Theseus danced it round the altar called Keraton, which is

constructed of horns (*kerata*) taken entirely from the left side of the head. He says that he also instituted athletic contests in Delos, and that the custom was then begun by him of giving a palm to the victors. (Plutarch, *Life of Theseus*)

Euripides in *Iphigenia Among the Taurians* (77-84) has Orestes describe the labyrinthine locutions his life has taken since the murder of Klytemnestra: how he had "fulfilled many twisting races" (δρόμους τε πολλοὺς ἐξέπλησα καμπίμους) getting nowhere until he asked Apollon "how I might come to the end of my wheel-driven madness and of my labors" (ἐλθὼν δέ σ' ἠρώτησα πῶς τροχηλάτου / μανίας ἂν ἔλθοιμ' ἐς τέλος πόνων τ' ἐμῶν).

Whereas in Bacchic Orphism it is to Dionysos and Kore that one turns for such release:

> The happy life, far from the roaming of generation, that is desired by those who in Orpheus are initiated to Dionysos and Kore and told 'to cease from the circle and enjoy respite from disgrace.' (Proklos, *Commentary on Plato's Timaeus* 3.296.7)

Similarly, in Plutarch this state of blessed deliverance comes after a period of circuitous wandering:

> When the soul comes to the point of death, it suffers something like those who participate in the great initiations (*teletai*). Therefore the word *teleutan* closely resembles the word *teleisthai* just as the act of dying resembles the act of being initiated. At first there are wanderings and toilsome running about in circles and journeys through the dark over uncertain roads and culs de sacs; then, just before the end, there are all kinds of terrors, with shivering, trembling, sweating, and utter amazement. After this, a strange and wonderful light meets the wanderer; he is admitted into clean and verdant meadows, where he discerns gentle voices, and choric dances, and the majesty of holy sounds and sacred visions. Here the now fully initiated is free, and walks at liberty like a crowned and dedicated victim, joining in the revelry. (*De Anima* fragment preserved in Stobaios *Florigelium* 120)

As it does in the gold leaf from Thurii:

> And I flew out from the hard and deeply-grievous circle, and stepped onto the crown with my swift feet, and slipped into the bosom of the Mistress, the Queen of the Underworld. Then I stepped out from the crown with my swift feet.

If the crown and circle remind you of Ariadne and the Labyrinth:

> The author of the *Cretica* says that when Liber came to Minos with the hope of lying with Ariadne he gave her this crown as a present. Delighted with it, she did not refuse the terms. It is said, too, to have been made of gold and Indian gems, and by its aid Theseus is thought to have come from the gloom of the Labyrinth to the day, for the gold and gems made a glow of light in the darkness. (Hyginus, *Astronomica* 2.5)

That is not accidental. In another of the gold leaves, once the stream of Lethe in the underworld has been passed, the thirsty soul is advised:

> You will find another one, from the Lake of Memory,
> cold water pouring forth; there are guards before it.
> They will ask you, with astute wisdom,
> what you are seeking in the darkness of murky Hades.
> "Who are you? Where are you from?"
> You tell them the entire truth.
> Say, "I am a child of Earth and Starry Sky. My name is Starry."

What you say to the guard is actually Ἀστέριος ὄνομα, "My name is Asterios." With this proclamation the initiate identifies himself with the bull of Minos – that sad, solitary creature trapped underground for the sins of his ancestors:

> He built a wooden cow on wheels, skinned a real cow, and sewed the contraption into the skin. And then, after placing Pasiphae inside, set it in a meadow where the bull normally grazed. The bull came up and had intercourse with it, as if with a real cow. Pasiphae gave birth to Asterios, who was called Minotauros. He had the face of a bull, but was otherwise human. Minos, following certain oracular instructions, kept him confined and under guard in the Labyrinth. (Apollodoros, *Bibliotheka* 3.11)

In Jorge Luis Borges' story "The House of Asterion" (from the collection *Labyrinths: Selected Stories and Other Writings*), the titular character has been wandering its circular passages in solitude for so long that he's lost his mind and nearly forgotten who he is:

> Of course, I am not without distractions. Like the ram about to charge, I run through the stone galleries until I fall dizzy to the floor. I crouch in the shadow of a pool or around a corner and pretend I am being followed. There are roofs from which I let

myself fall until I am bloody. At any time I can pretend to be asleep, with my eyes closed and my breathing heavy. (Sometimes I really sleep, sometimes the color of day has changed when I open my eyes.) But of all the games, I prefer the one about the other Asterion. I pretend that he comes to visit me and that I show him my house. With great obeisance I say to him "Now we shall return to the first intersection" or "Now we shall come out into another courtyard" Or "I knew you would like the drain" or "Now you will see a pool that was filled with sand" or "You will soon see how the cellar branches out". Sometimes I make a mistake and the two of us laugh heartily.

Not only have I imagined these games, I have also meditated on the house. All parts of the house are repeated many times, any place is another place. There is no one pool, courtyard, drinking trough, manger; the mangers, drinking troughs, courtyards pools are fourteen in number. The house is the same size as the world; or rather it is the world. However, by dint of exhausting the courtyards with pools and dusty gray stone galleries I have reached the street and seen the temple of the Axes and the sea. I did not understand this until a night vision revealed to me that the seas and temples are also fourteen in number. Everything is repeated many times, fourteen times, but two things in the world seem to be repeated only once: above, the intricate sun; below Asterion. Perhaps I have created the stars and the sun and this enormous house, but I no longer remember.

Every nine years nine men enter the house so that I may deliver them from evil. I hear their steps or their voices in the depths of the stone galleries and I run joyfully to find them. The ceremony lasts a few minutes. They fall one after another without my having to bloody my hands. They remain where they fell and their bodies help distinguish one gallery from another. I do not know who they are, but I know that one of them prophesied, at the moment of his death, that someday my redeemer would come. Since then my loneliness does not pain me, because I know my redeemer lives and he will finally rise above the dust. If my ear could capture all the sounds of the world, I should hear his steps. I hope he will take me to a place with fewer galleries fewer doors. What will my redeemer be like? I ask myself. Will he be a bull or a man? Will he perhaps be a bull with the face of a man? Or will he be like me?

That double, that redeemer that Asterion so longs for, is Dionysos – who in Naples was represented as a bull with a man's face (Pighius, *Hercules prodocius* 329). He comes many times in the story, but Asterion thinks him only his own reflection and so remains trapped.

Finally, it is Persephone who finds her way to him, led there by Ariadne. Borges' story concludes:

> The morning sun reverberated from the bronze sword. There was no longer even a vestige of blood. "Would you believe it, Ariadne?" said Theseus, "The Minotaur scarcely defended himself."

This makes Ariadne not betrayer but savior of her brother, releasing him from the grievous circle so that he may run free in the groves and meadows of Persephone with the other *mystai* and *bakchoi*.

Rhombos the Bullroarer

Clement of Alexandria calls this Toy ῥόμβος, which the scholiast felt needed the following clarification:

> The *rhombos* is a bit of wood to which a string is tied, and it is whirled round and round at initiation-rites to make a whirring sound.

This is because the word *rhombos* had a wide range of usage in antiquity. The Liddell & Scott *Greek-English Lexicon* provides the following definitions:

1. *bull-roarer*, instrument whirled round on the end of a string, used in the mysteries, "ῥόμβου θ᾽ εἱλισσομένα κύκλιος ἔνοσις αἰθερία" E.Hel.1362, cf. *Archyt.1*, Theoc.2.30; as a boy's toy, *AP*6.309 (*Leon.*), *Orph.Fr.*31.29, *Fr.*34, M.Ant.5.36; defined as ξυλήφιον, οὗ ἐξῆπται τὸ σπαρτίον, καὶ ἐν ταῖς τελεταῖς ἐδονεῖτο, ἵνα ῥοιζῇ *SchClem.Al.Protr.*2.17.2

2. *magic wheel*, spun alternately in each direction by the torsion of two cords passed through two holes in it, used as a love-charm, Luc.DMeretr. 4.5; called ἴυγξ in Theoc.2.17, *AP*5.204; Lat. *rhombus*, Prop.2.28.35, Ov.*Am.*1.8.7.

3. *tambourine* or *kettle-drum*, used in the worship of Rhea and of Dionysus, Ar.Fr.303, Diog.Ath.1.3, A.R. 1.1139, *AP*6.165 (*Phal.*); "ῥύμβος ξύλινος ἐπίχρυσος" *IG*22.1456.49, cf. *1517.207*

4. *membrum virile*, *PLond.1821.164*.

5. *rhombus, lozenge*, i.e. a four-sided figure with all the sides, but only the opposite angles, equal, *Arist.Mech.854b16*, Euc.1 *Def.* 22. a figure composed of two cones on opposite sides of the same base, *Archim.Sph.Cyl.1.26*, al.

6. *a species of fish*, of which *turbot* and *brill* are varieties, so called from its rhomblike shape, *Nausicr.2.13*; Ῥωμαῖοι καλοῦσι τὴν ψῆτταν ῥ. Ath.7.330b, cf. ψῆττα.

7. *surgical bandage*, so called from its shape, Hp. *Off.*7, *Heliod.* ap. *Orib.48.20.14*.

8. *pattern of the same shape*, in weaving cloth, *Democr.Eph.1*; διαπλοκὴ ῥόμβων Aristeas 74.

While some of these other meanings are indeed interesting, it is unlikely that the Titans gave the child-god a fish or a lozenge-shaped piece of surgical bandage to play with.

But a bull-roarer, now that'd catch his attention!

It certainly caught the Indians by surprise when one of Dionysos' Bakchai turned her improvised *rhombos* into a weapon:

> Stesichore, rich in clusters of grapes, jumped into the fray and scattered a tribe of enemies with her manbreaking *rhombos*, whirling the loudly-clashing bronze over her head. (*Dionysiaka* 14.400-402)

We learn how this Stesichore made the disconcerting sounds with her *rhombos* in a fragment from Archytas of Tarentum:

> That high notes are in swift motion, low notes in slow motion, has become clear to us from many examples, such as the 'whirlers' (*rhomboi*) which are swung round at the mysteries: if they are whirled gently, they give out a low note, if vigorously, a high note.

The *rhombos* also signifies a sudden and powerful Dionysiac epiphany in the *Helen* of Euripides:

> *Chorus member 1*: The power of the magnificent adorned cape made of deerskin is mighty!
> *Chorus member 2*: So is the green ivy that winds itself around the sacred thyrsus!

Chorus member 1: So is the din of the bull-roarer that spins about the air!
Chorus member 2: So is that of the Mother's tresses as the wind takes them when she's dancing the all night vigils of Bacchus. All through the night, beneath the radiance of the moon they dance. (1359-1363)

Technically in this passage Euripides describes the whirling of the *rhombos* as κύκλιος ένοσις αίθερία, "rotating earthquake in the air" which finds parallels in Nonnos' description of the *rhombos* as μυκήτωρ, "bellower" whose sound he compares to thunder (*Dionysiaka* 41.81) and this fragment from Aischylos' play *Edonai*:

> ... even the sound that wakes to frenzy. Another, with brass-bound cymbals, raises a clang ... the twang shrills; the unseen, unknown, bull-voiced mimes in answer bellow fearfully, while the *rhombos'* echo, like that of subterranean thunder, rolls along inspiring a mighty terror. (frag. 27)

Which likely coincides with the arrival of Dionysos before the frightened and insane king Lykourgos, who up to that point had been resisting the introduction of the Bacchic cult into Thrace.

None of this is accidental.

Olga Levaniou (*The Toys of Dionysos*) asserts that the *rhombos* was used to frighten initiates, "its effect augmented by the fact that when it is in motion the startling sound of the *rhombos* seems to come out of nowhere, έξ άφανούς, like thunder." She then goes on to note that fear and confusion are a well-attested feature of initiations, and cites Plutarch's testimony that "all kinds of fearful things, terror and trembling and sweat and wonder" (fragment 178) were part of the process as well as Proklos' description of initiates being "full of astonishment and fear" (*on Republic* 2.108.21-22).

Digging deeper, Olga interprets what the *rhombos* may have meant to initiates:

> It could evoke specific parts of the code of the mysteries: the initiate's fear, the bellowing bull, thunder and lightning, earthquake, and cosmic confusion. In the *Edonians*, the "mimes with voices like bulls" appear in the immediate proximity of the earthquake, while in the *Bacchae* it is precisely when the earthquake shakes the house of Pentheus, and Semele's tomb ignites as if by lightning, that Pentheus first begins to confuse Dionysos with a bull (618-624). If this combination of thunder, earthquake, and the bull's appearance was part of the mysteries, then the *rhombos* is likely to have been used at this stage of the *telete* and to point back to it as a *symbolon*. In *Prometheus Bound* (1082-1088) thunder is again

compared to the bellowing of cattle, the earth quakes, and the context is precisely the mania afflicting the bovine Io. Although the *rhombos* is not mentioned, there are *stromboi* ("whirlwinds"), part of a sudden and fearful storm which signals the renewed attack of madness after a brief reprieve. As Padel has shown, meteorological metaphors are fundamental to the Greek understanding of madness and fit in with the contemporary medical and biological ideas about fluids (or floods) and "breaths" (or winds). The semantic field of the spinning toys overlaps with this meteorological metaphor, and as a result, the motion associated with mania is often circular. In the *Bacchae*, for example, the maenads are described as ἑλισόμεναι "whirling." (569)

Strobilos the Top

The Orphic poem cited by Clement of Alexandria names this Toy κωνος (*kōnos*) while the Christian apologist amends it to στρόβιλος (*stróbilos*) – both are referring to a top, though like a lot of people I originally assumed that two Toys were indicated, the other being a pinecone.

It makes sense, after all.

Pinecones were highly regarded for their fertilizing power:

> To be able to copulate a lot grind up fifty tiny pinecones with 2 ozs. of sweet wine and two pepper grains and drink it. (*PGM* VII.184-5)

Souls start out as pinecones:

> For the soul, proceeding from a round figure, which is the only divine form, is extended into the form of a cone in going forth. (Macrobius, *In Somnia Scipionis* 12)

Dionysos was placed in a bed of pine by his aunts:

> Ino, daughter of Agenor, reared the infant Bakchos and first gave her breast to the son of Zeus, and Autonoë likewise and Agave joined in nursing him; not, as it happened, in the baleful halls of Athamas, but on the mountain which at that time men called by the name Meros. For greatly fearing the mighty spouse of Zeus and dreading the tyrant Pentheus, son of Echion, they laid the holy child in a coffer of pine and covered it with fawn-skins and wreathed it with clusters of the vine, in a grotto where round the child they

danced the mystic dance and beat drums and clashed cymbals in their hands, to veil the cries of the infant. (*Oppian, Cynegetica 4. 230 ff*)

Torches used in Bacchic worship were often made of pine:

> The leader of our revel
> holds the torch high
> blazing flame of pine
> and sweet smoke like Syrian incense.
> (Euripides, *Bakchai* 183-86)

This is the tree that Pentheus was killed in:

> They say that Pentheus treated Dionysos spitefully, his crowning outrage being that he went to Kithairon to spy upon the women, and climbing up a tall pinetree beheld what was done. When the women detected Pentheus, they immediately dragged him down, and joined in tearing him, living as he was, limb from limb. Afterwards, as the Corinthians say, the Pythian priestess commanded them by an oracle to discover that tree and to worship it equally with the god. For this reason they have made images from the tree. (*Pausanias, Description of Greece 2. 2.6-7*)

And most importantly, pinecones adorn the tip of thyrsoi, the ivy-woven wands that are a ubiquitous part of the Dionysiac costume. They were even first presented to him, according to Olympiodoros, by the Titans along with the Toys:

> The thyrsos is a symbol of a forming anew of the material and parted substance from its scattered condition; on this account it is a Titanic plant. This it was customary to extend to Dionysos instead of his paternal scepter; and through this they called him down into our partial nature. Indeed, the Titans are thyrsos-bearers; and Prometheus concealed fire in a thyrsos or fennel stalk; after which he is considered as bringing celestial light into generation, or leading the soul into the body, or calling forth divine illumination, the whole being ungenerated, into generated existence. Hence Sokrates called the multitude thyrsos-bearers Orphically as living according to a Titanic life." (*Commentary on Plato's Phaido*)

But alas, the scholars are unequivocal – *kōnos* is a top.

> Over a century ago Lobeck, in a passage of astonishing learning (*Agl.* 699 ff.), was prepared to show that in spite of the attempts to

attach an original mystical significance to these objects, every one of them was in origin nothing but what the story made them out to be---children's toys. The strongest support to a contrary theory was furnished by the words *konos* and *rhombos* in the Orphic lines. The former means, in the first place, a pine cone, and pine cones were carried by the worshippers in Dionysiac processions on the tips of their wands, the *thyrsoi*. The latter means a bull-roarer, an instrument which when whirled around the head produces a noise, and is or has been used in the religious ceremonies of primitive peoples in many lands. It happens, however, that both words also mean spinning-top, and Lobeck went so far as to discover a passage in a Greek writer which explained exactly the difference between the two, for every small boy, it seemed knew that a *konos* was not the same as a *rhombos*. One was the kind you whipped, and the other was not. We shall soon come to some evidence, unknown to Lobeck, that in the story of the divine child it was spinning-tops that were in question. (W.K.C. Guthrie, *Orpheus and Greek Religion* pg 121)

Even more emphatically, Olga Levaniou, whose *Toys of Dionysos* I've cited previously, states:

It is preferable to understand the *kōnos* in the Orphic lines as a spinning top, and specifically as a whipping top, as suggested by Guthrie. The spinning top is more appropriate to a list of toys, and the Orphic lines are explicitly introduced as describing toys, not ritual implements. Moreover, Arnobius in his unambiguous Latin says nothing at all about pine-cones, but ascribes to Orpheus a mention of *turbines* and *volubiles rotulae*, both spinning toys. This means that Arnobius understood *kōnos* in the Orphic lines to refer to a spinning top, not a pine-cone. Arnobius's list contains two spinning toys. If *kōnos*/ *strobilos* means "top," then each of the other lists also contains two such toys: *kōnos* and *rhombos* in Orpheus and on the Gurob papyrus, and *rhombos* and *strobilos* in Clement. Finally, the very grouping of the words points to the spinning top. In two of our three Greek sources (the Gurob papyrus and Orpheus) *kōnos* appears next to *rhombos*, the bull-roarer. There is no particular reason why the *rhombos* should repeatedly appear next to a pine-cone, but there is a good reason why two different kinds of spinning toys should go together. Given the scarcity of our sources, the fact that this pairing of *kōnos* and *rhombos* occurs twice may indicate that it is both a stable set of toys and a stable phrase.

Which naturally begs the question *why*? Why do each of our sources include two such similar Toys in their lists? And why is the presence of these two a constant when other Toys may be added or omitted at random?

It's because they are variations on a theme, a theme that was central to the Bacchic Orphic mysteries; and each of these Toys expressed that theme differently or rather from a different perspective and stage of the initiatory process. The theme that they share is madness.

Rhombos is the initial encounter with madness – a sudden and unsettling storm that engulfs us and penetrates our defenses, while Kōnos (or Stróbilos) begins within and spirals outward.

But first there's the sting, the bite, the blow; largely unnoticed until the poison is already seeping through your veins.

Virgil evocatively portrayed this in his account of the Bacchant Queen Amata:

> But she sees her lord Latinus resolute, her words
> an effort vain; and through her body spreads
> the Fury's deeply venomed viper-sting.
> Then, woe-begone, by dark dreams goaded on,
> she wanders aimless, fevered and unstrung
> along the public ways; as oft one sees
> beneath the twisted whips a leaping top
> sped in long spirals through a palace-close
> by lads at play: obedient to the thong,
> it weaves wide circles in the gaping view
> of its small masters, who admiring see
> the whirling boxwood made a living thing
> under their lash. (*Aeneid* 7.385)

In doing so he was drawing on an ancient metaphorical tradition – for instance, in Pindar's *Pythian* 4, Medea is compelled by a "whip of persuasion" (μάστιγι Πειθούς), and in Aischylos' *Prometheus Bound* (682-683), Io envisages the gadfly (*oistros*) which stings her as a whip (μάστιγι Θεία γήν πρό γής ἐλαύνομαι, "I am driven with a divine whip from land to land"), and even as far back as Homer's *Iliad* 6.135 the nurses of "mad Dionysos" run and scatter under the blows of a cow-whip or goad (θεινόμεναι βουπλήγι). The sting of this insect is typically compared to a whip, and the word *myops* can in fact mean, literally, "goad" or "whip." The gadfly is a standard feature in descriptions of madness – so standard that the word *oistros* itself comes to mean "madness" and produces several derivatives with this meaning. In Euripides' *Bakchai* (32-33), Dionysos spurs (literally "gadflies") the women out of their houses (ἐκ δόμων ὤστρησ ἐγώ μανίας) and the crowd of women is described as "gadflied" by him (οἰστροπηθείς Διονύσῳ, 119). The maenads themselves are described as οἰστροπλῆγας, "oistros-struck" (979, 1229), just as Io is both οἰστροπλήξ and οἰστροδίνητος "oistros-spun" in *Prometheus Bound* (589, 681).

This was, however, a metaphorical tradition rooted in cultic reality.

In Arcadian Alea Pausanias observed:

> In honor of Dionysos they celebrate every other year a festival called Skiereia, and at this festival in obedience to an oracle from Delphoi women are flogged. (Pausanias, *Description of Greece* 8.23.1)

Which was also an element of the Agrionia festival:

> Proitos had daughters, Lysippe, Iphinoe, and Iphianassa, by Stheneboea. When these damsels were grown up, they went mad, according to Hesiod, because they would not accept the rites of Dionysos, but according to Akusilaos, because they disparaged the wooden image of Hera. In their madness they roamed over the whole Argive land, and afterwards, passing through Arcadia and the Peloponnese, they ran through the desert in the most disorderly fashion. But Melampos, son of Amythaon by Idomene, daughter of Abas, being a seer and the first to devise the cure by means of drugs and purifications, promised to cure the maidens if he should receive the third part of the sovereignty. When Proitos refused to pay so high a fee for the cure, the maidens raved more than ever, and besides that, the other women raved with them; for they also abandoned their houses, destroyed their own children, and flocked to the desert. Not until the evil had reached a very high pitch did Proitos consent to pay the stipulated fee, and Melampos promised to effect a cure whenever his brother Bias should receive just so much land as himself. Fearing that, if the cure were delayed, yet more would be demanded of him, Proitos agreed to let the physician proceed on these terms. So Melampos, taking with him the most stalwart of the young men, chased the women in a bevy from the mountains to Sicyon with shouts and a sort of frenzied dance. In the pursuit Iphinoe, the eldest of the daughters, expired; but the others were lucky enough to be purified and so to recover their wits. Proitos gave them in marriage to Melampos and Bias, and afterwards begat a son, Megapenthes. (Apollodoros, *Bibliotheka* 2.2-3.1)

Clement (*Protreptikos* 2.16.3) reports that *boukoloi* carried sacred ox-goads and Hesychios notes the word θυρσπλῆγες meaning:

> thyrsos-struck: those transported during Bacchic revelry.

Walter Burkert records other instances of Bacchic whipping scenes:

> There remains the intriguing depiction in the Villa of the Mysteries of what is no doubt a flagellation scene. A kneeling girl, keeping her head in the lap of a seated woman and shutting her eyes, the seated woman grasping her hands and drawing back the garment from the kneeling girl's bare back, while a sinister-looking female behind is raising a rod – these are all quite realistic details of caning. But the threatening figure wielding the rod had black wings; she is not from this world but rather an allegorical personality. Some allusions to flogging in Bacchic contexts have been collected, from Plautus to late sarcophagi. On these we find Pan or satyr-boys being disciplined with a sandal, but the situation and the iconography are quite different. On the other hand, madness is described as feeling the strokes of a whip as early as in Attic tragedy; Lyssa, as 'frenzy' personified, appears with a whip in vase painting, and in any event *mania* is the special province of Dionysus. Not even Aphrodite would disdain a *sublime flagellum* to make an arrogant girl move to her command, as Horace suggests. This would dissolve the flagellation scene into pure symbolism; at the critical moment, with a stroke, divine madness will take possession of the initiate, and the kneeling girl, changed into a true bacchant, will rise and move freely in frenzied dance just like the other dancer next to this scene. Yet symbolism does not exclude ritual practice, and there are suggestions that one form of purification, *catharsis*, could in fact be flogging. Once more art has succeeded in remaining intentionally ambiguous as to what actually occurred in the mysteries. (*Ancient Mystery Cults* 103-4)

Just like Vergil's Amata, in Ps.-Lucian's *Onos* (42.20) the narrator is beaten and compares himself to a spinning top:

> For many of those inside took up canes and, without my expecting it, for I could see nothing, they struck me with incessant blows standing around me, so that I suddenly began to spin under their blows like a top.

Which gives us a sense of what Kōnos-Stróbilos signifies and how it differs from Rhombos.

Olga Levaniou elaborates:

> The whipping top brings to mind both fast, circular motion and the whipping effect, but there is a difference between the two toys: while the *rhombos* whips, the top suffers the whipping. Like the

maenads and the crazed cows (such as Io), the whipping top is hit and sent spinning, and the action of driving it can be described by the verb ἐλαύνω, also used of driving cattle. The image of the top thus seems to invite the thought of whipping and as a symbolon of the mysteries, captures not only the whipping and circular motion, but the suddenness of the attack, the confusion, fear, and pain of the neophyte, and even the contrast between the calm initiators and the frantic novices. The spinning and whipping are typical of mania in general, but as a symbolon of the mysteries, the top points more concretely to manic experiences as seen through the visual, acoustic, and emotional code of the *teletai*.

Krotala the Rattle

Iulius Firmicus Maternus provides an abbreviated account of the Toys, mentioning only a wondrously wrought mirror and rattles. Judging by their ubiquity in Dionysiac scenes, the rattles meant by the Latin apologist were the κρόταλα, whose invention Clement of Alexandria attributes to the Sicilians. William Smith describes the krótala as follows:

> The simplest form was probably a couple of shells or potsherds pierced with holes and strung together (λεπάδας δὲ πετρῶν ἀποκόπτοντες κρεμβαλιάψουσι, Hermipp. fragm. 29 Meineke; κογχύλια καὶ ὄστρακα, Didymus ap. Ath. 14.636 d, quoted also by the Scholiast on Aristoph. *Frogs* 1305; testarum crepitus, Juv. 11.170; σκεῦός τι ἐξ ὀστράκου, Eustath. ad Il. 11.160). Some writers explain ὄστρακα as though the *crotalum* were actually moulded in earthenware; but this seems less likely. Brass and wood are also mentioned as materials (κρόταλα χαλκοῦ, Eur. Cycl. 204, cf. Mart. 11.16; cava buxa, Propert. 5.8, 42; Eustath. l.c.); and a split reed or cane (ὁ σχιψόμενος κάλαμος, Schol. Aristoph. Cl. 260; Suidas). Altogether the *crotalum* cannot have differed much from the castanets now so often heard as an accompaniment to certain kinds of vocal music. (*A Dictionary of Greek and Roman Antiquities*)

Krótala belonged to the third category of instruments in Aristoxenos of Tarentum's tripartite system consisting of strings, winds and καθαπτά "those that resound when held and touched upon," or our modern percussion. This last class was singled out for derision by Clement of

Alexandria who forbid the use of percussion instruments in Christian worship because they led to "improper frivolity, indecency, crude gesticulations and insanity" (*Paidagagos* 2.4).

Discussing the relationship between percussion instruments and Dionysos, Layne Redmond writes:

> Pyrrhic dances set to frame drumming were also incorporated into the religious festivals and dramatic theater. This puts percussion at the root of the development of western theater. Knowing the widespread and ancient connection between drumming and dance forms, and that Greek dancers were highly identified with the frame drum, cymbals, and *krotalas*, it is hard to visualize Greek dance developing first to melodic instruments with percussion added later. (*Percussion Instruments of Ancient Greece*)

The Pyrrhic dance was a martial dance with strong Dionysian associations, according to Athenaios:

> But the Pyrrhic dance continues in use only among the Lacedaemonians who consider it a sort of preparation for war. All who are more than five years old in Sparta learn to dance the Pyrrhic dance, which appears to be a sort of Dionysiac dance, for the dancers carry thyrsi like spears and they point and dart canes at one another, and carry torches. And in their dances, they portray Dionysos and the Indians, and the story of Pentheus: and they require for the Pyrrhic dance the most beautiful and stirring of tunes. (*Deipnosphistai* 631a-b)

Interestingly, the invention of this dance was credited to Phalanx, the brother of Arachne, a point which will prove significant momentarily:

> And Theophilos, of the school of Zenodotos, records that in Attica there were two siblings; Phalanx, a boy and the girl was named Arachne. They were tutored by Athene, Phalanx learning the arts of war from her and Arachne the art of weaving. However the goddess came to abhor them since they had intercourse with one another, transforming them into animals destined to be eaten by their own offspring. (Scholiast on Nikander's *Theriaka* 12.a)

Of all the percussion instruments known to the ancient Greeks, the krótala was perhaps most strongly associated with Dionysos, according to Layne Redmond:

> Although there is a depiction of the goddess Artemis playing the *krotalas*, these clackers most frequently appear in Dionysian dance

scenes. In these scenes they are played by male satyrs and women maenads and often accompanied by double flute players. In the Beazley Vase Collection, the *krotalas* appear on 569 Greek vases from the Black figured (app. 610–510 BCE) and Red figured (app. 530–400 BCE) periods, which means they appear earlier than the frame drums, which do not appear until the Red-figured period. They are played by both men and women, but there are noticeably more women players than men. Most often the performer is dancing and plays a set of *krotalas* in each hand, but sometimes they play only one set in one hand. In some symposium scenes male youths are shown lounging on couches while playing the *krotalas*. Although the *krotalas* appear more frequently than any other percussion instrument on the vases, deities are most often depicted in sculptural form holding the frame drum. (ibid)

Nor is this something limited just to the iconographic record. Herodotos describes their use during a festival characterized by "great sacrifices, during which more wine is drunk than in the whole year besides" as follows:

> Some of the women make a noise with rattles, others play flutes all the way, while the rest of the women, and the men, sing and clap their hands; still others dance, and some stand up and lift their skirts. (*Histories* 2.60)

A fragment of Catallus reads:

> There sounds the clang of the cymbals, there echo the tympanons, there the Phrygian flutist plays upon his deep-sounding, twisted reed. There the Maenads, adorned with ivy, toss their heads wildly and play the castanets.

Just like in the Bacchic *thiasos* described by Tacitus:

> Messalina meanwhile, more wildly profligate than ever, was celebrating in mid-autumn a representation of the vintage in her new home. The presses were being trodden; the vats were overflowing; women girt with skins were dancing and playing the castanets, as Bacchanals dance in their worship or their frenzy. Messalina with flowing hair shook the thyrsus, and Silius at her side, crowned with ivy and wearing the buskin, moved his head to some lascivious chorus. (*Annals* 11.31.2)

Clement's observation that krótala were invented in Sicily is significant, for the region of Magna Graecia was also where other Dionysian percussion instruments developed, such as tympana that incorporated krótala-like rattles:

> The tympana represented in Apulian pottery were much more elaborate than the drums pictured in Attic pots, being almost a new instrument: the membranes were ornate with concentric geometric or floral motives and dots; decorative ribbons hang from the drum; sometimes they seem to have small rattles; their size varied from very small to very large, on average reaching 60 cm diameter. According to Di Giulio 1991, the Apulian drum's originality "demonstrates a level of cultural independence of the indigenous population." The tympanon became a more complex instrument and became an expression of the regional popularity of the cult of Dionysus, while the use of the rectangular sistrum, known in South Italy and Sicily since the 8th century, spread all over Magna Graecia, imposing itself as an Apulian cultural symbol. (Fábio Vergara Cerqueira, *Iconographical Representations of Musical Instruments in Apulian Vase-Painting as Ethnical Signs: Intercultural Greek-Indigenous Relations in Magna Graecia in the 5th and 4th Centuries B.C.*)

The Apulian sistrum differed significantly from sistra found in Greece, but had some resemblance to those used in Egypt and the Levant, as Fábio Vergara Cerqueira goes on to describe:

> The third case is the so-called 'Apulian sistrum.' There is no trace of this instrument in any source from mainland Greece, written, iconographical or archaeological. It was a percussion instrument shaped by two bars connected by a varied number of crossbars, with small bells and rattles on the ends that sounded when shaken. We cannot be sure of its name, although some authors have tended to identify it as the *platage* mentioned by Archytas of Tarentum (Smith 1976, 137). Others named it 'Apulian sistrum', by analogy with the Egyptian instrument of Hathor and Isis, and adopted the supposition that it had an Apulian origin because of its frequency in images on Apulian pottery. Recent studies based in South Italian archaeological findings and in similar Mesopotamian iconographical testimonies indicate, however, that it was probably known for a few centuries in Sicily and South Italy thanks to the exchange of oriental merchandise, probably with the Phoenicians. (ibid)

We get a sense of what these rattles may have meant in a cultic context from Plutarch:

> The sistrum intimates to us that all things ought to be agitated and shook (σείεσθαι), and not to suffer rest from motion, and when they begin to grow drowsy and to droop they have to be roused up and awakened. For they tell us that the sistrum averts and frightens off Typhon, insinuating hereby that as corruption locks up and fixes Nature's course, so generation again resolves and excites it by means of motion. Moreover, as the sistrum hath its upper part convex, so its circumference contains the four things that are shaken; for that part of the world also which is liable to generation and corruption is contained by the sphere of the moon, but all things are moved and changed in it by means of the four elements: fire, earth, water, and air. (*On Isis and Osiris* 63)

Katerina Kolotourou goes further in discussing the religious significance of percussion instruments, the rattle in particular:

> In ritual, the percussive action and performance may thus enact in a physical manner the fierceness that impels the dynamic transition from one state to the other, in the same way that the mythical dismemberment of Dionysos conveys the message of destruction and restoration in a narrative form. [...] Through their musical performance the participants in ritual aspire to connect with the divine powers which have the ability to reconcile death with birth, elimination with growth, peril with existence, and ultimately chaos with order. There is no more explicit manifestation of the communion with the divine than that of divine possession, which is an integral part of the rituals of mystery cults. The importance of music and dance in reaching the state of *enthousiasmos*, whereby the worshippers are possessed by the divine spirit, is well known. In Plato's account of telestic mania it is maintained that through the disorder of their ecstatic dancing the ritual participants will be "healed" and re-establish their union with the cosmos, which is ultimately orderly and harmonious. When imaging divine musical performance, it is usually earth goddesses such as Kybele, her variants Mother of the Gods and Rhea with the associated Kouretes, as well as Aphrodite-Astarte that take on percussion. Similarly, Aphrodite brings on her tympana and cymbals to entertain the distressed Demeter in a passage from Euripides' *Helen* (1338–1352), while a scene on a red-figure volute crater of the Dinos Painter shows Demeter or Ariadne clashing the cymbals next to Dionysos as they attend the return of Hephaistos accompanied by the dancing thiasos. No doubt, these renderings of divine percussionists emanate from the established cultic contexts where the instruments were played. But the idea of a divine precedent for percussive activity, on

which mortals would model their own performances, is a mythological analogue to an ingrained belief in the powers of such actions to generate life and thus to reinstate cosmic order, as the performative example of the *anodos* clearly demonstrates. Order and disorder as well as destruction and creation are periodically alternating states, the temporal patterning of which structures the natural as well as the human cycle. The Hesiodic religious model presents a world where order results from strife and it designates divine powers to be as much destructive as they are restoring. This duality similarly characterizes percussive actions that encode man's earliest experiences of generation and elimination. Percussive enactment, therefore, can be understood as a means to imitate ritually the divine, realizing through human agency the link between the polar opposites of creation and destruction. (*Musical Rhythms From The Cradle To The Grave*)

This is why Strabo felt:

> Mousikē, which includes dancing as well as rhythm and melody, by the delight it affords and by its artistic beauty, brings us in touch with the divine. (*Geography* 10.3.9)

And Aristides Quintilianus felt that music could cure mental illness by bringing on divine *mania*:

> Our discussion makes it clear that the first and most natural source of melody is divine possession. When the soul has sunk down towards this world through its abandonment of wisdom, falling into mere ignorance and forgetfulness through the torpor of the body, and becoming filled with confusion and excitement, it becomes temporarily delirious and subject to what amounts to a lunatic frenzy. Those who are insane may be soothed with melody: either the patients must themselves appease the irrational element through imitations of their own (this course is appropriate for those whose characters are savage and bestial), or they must avert the dreadful affliction through the use of their eyes and ears (if they are educated and their nature more orderly.) Hence, they say, there is a degree of reason behind Bacchic rites and similar initiations: they serve to cleanse away, with their songs and dances and games, the frenetic excitedness to which foolish folk have become subject by their way of life, or merely by chance. (*De musica* 25)

Which of course brings us into the realm of maenadism, which had a strong presence in Magna Graecia as Andromache Karanika writes in

Ecstasis in Healing: Practices in Southern Italy and Greece from Antiquity to the Present:

The state of maenadism did not consist of a permanent situation but rather was a periodic and recurrent phenomenon that did not demand any further participation in the Dionysian cult. Evidence from the Bacchic revels, involving both men and women, that caused a scandal in 186 B.C. in Rome has not only helped us understand some of the aspects of the cult, but has also been greatly misleading. The maenads of Magna Graecia survive in artistic representations on vases from southern Italy. One of the most significant sources, however, is a fragment of Aristoxenus of Tarentum from the mid-fourth century B.C. who gives information about the performance of women from Rhegium and Locri Epizephyrii. He describes how women suddenly are overcome by *ecstasis*, while in the midst of dining or some other activity. The symptoms seemed to be of the same periodic, non-permanent type proper to tarantism today. They are not strictly related to a Dionysian cult or ritual maenadism as we know it from other extant sources, but a maenadic ambiance might be assumed. What is more interesting is the origin of the cure that was prescribed by the Delphic oracle. As Henrichs remarks,

> The cure prescribed by the Delphic oracle consisted in the singing of paeans during spring-time. The mysterious voice which unbalanced the women, and their sudden and agitated escape from their normal way of life, highlighted by the "Bacchic verb" "jump," have close parallels in Euripides' *Bacchant Women*, 1078–1094. The Delphic cure is similar to the homeopathic treatment which the Proetids received from the prophet Melampus.

Dodds, in his influential study of the "irrational" in ancient Greece, distinguishes among four different types of madness: prophetic madness associated with Apollo; telestic or ritual madness associated with Dionysus; poetic madness inspired by the Muses, and erotic madness induced by Aphrodite and Dionysus. In a sense, the kind of ecstatic dance performance that has been attested to in southern Italy could be seen as an example of ritual madness, enhanced with erotic and certainly poetic overtones, as the song is the cure.

Musical cures of this sort go all the way back to Orpheus:

> In Pieria frenzied female worshipers of Dionysos were tearing apart the bodies of sheep and goats and performing many other violent acts; they turned to the mountains to spend their days there. When they failed to return to their homes, the townspeople, fearing for the safety of their wives and daughters, summoned Orpheus and asked him to devise a plan to get the women down from the mountain. Orpheus performed appropriate sacrificial rites to the god Dionysos and then by playing his lyre led the frenzied Bacchants down from the mountain. But as the women descended they held in their hands various kinds of trees. To the men who watched on that occasion the pieces of wood seemed wondrous. So they said, 'By playing his lyre Orpheus is bringing the very forest down from the mountain.' And from this the myth was created. (Palaiphatos, *Peri Apiston* 33)

And Pythagoras:

> While his friends were in good health Pythagoras always conversed with them; if they were sick, he nursed them; if they were afflicted in mind, he solaced them, some by incantations and magic charms, others by music. He had prepared songs for the diseases of the body, by singing which he cured the sick. He had also some that caused forgetfulness of sorrow, mitigation of anger, and destruction of lust. (Porphyry, *Life of Pythagoras* 33)

To the ancients music was able to cure more than just psychosomatic ailments, as Theophrastos and Demokritos observed in fragments preserved in Aulus Gellius:

> I ran across the statement very recently in the book of Theophrastus *On Inspiration* that many men have believed and put their belief on record, that when gouty pains in the hips are most severe, they are relieved if a flute-player plays soothing measures. That snake-bites are cured by the music of the flute, when played skilfully and melodiously, is also stated in a book of Democritus, entitled *On Deadly Infections*, in which he shows that the music of the flute is medicine for many ills that flesh is heir to. So very close is the connection between the bodies and the minds of men, and therefore between physical and mental ailments and their remedies. (*Attic Nights* 4.13)

Which reminds one naturally of tarantism, a phenomenon that developed in the Apulian region where Bacchic cults had been prevalent in antiquity:

The spider which was held responsible for tarantism was a mythical creature which did not correspond to any arachnid of modern zoology. Instead, the taranta assembled the characteristics of several different species of spider into a mythical whole. Different colours were attributed to the spiders – principally red, green and black – and the 'bite' of each respective spider caused different behaviour in the victim. Those bit by red spiders displayed martial, heroic behaviour; those bit by green spiders displayed eroticised behaviour; and those bitten by black spiders were fascinated by funerary paraphernalia. Furthermore, each colour spider had its own repertoire of musical figures and dances: for example, those bitten by a green spider would only dance to a tarantella tune associated with the green spider. Finally, the victims of the spider's bite were fascinated by pieces of cloth with the appropriate colour. Thus, during the course of an exorcism different tarantella tunes were played and different coloured clothes were given to the victim in order to determine which spider possesses her. Only the appropriate tarantella tune, the appropriate colour and the appropriate dance would cure the victim – at least for the time being, until the affliction reoccured a year later. Music serves at once as diagnosis and therapy. Rather than the result of the bite of an actual spider, tarantism was a mythical-ritual experience which was modelled on the medical symptoms of the actual bite of a poisonous spider. Examining parallels in ethnography and folklore, De Martino found structural similarities between tarantism and Afro-Mediterranean and Afro-American (voodoo) possession cults. Furthermore, De Martino found antecedents to this religious formation in classical Greek mythology and rituals. (R. from quotidian banality)

This is particularly driven home in a letter from Domenico Sangenito to Antonio Bulifon:

> The *tarantati* want ribbons, chains, precious garments, and when they are brought they receive them with inexplicable joy, and with great reverence they thank the person who brought them. All of the aforementioned items are placed in an orderly fashion along the pen where the dancers make use of one or another item from time to time, according to the impulses the attack gives them. [...] In the castle of Motta di Montecorvino I had the occasion to see five *tarantati* dance at the same time and inside of the same stockade: they were four ploughmen and a beautiful country lass. Each had taken an alias, from among the names of ancient kings, no less. They treated each other in such a way that reciprocal affection was

observed, and compliments were reiterated to the great admiration of the spectators. They happily performed the usual course of the dance over three days; the last evening, before taking leave, they politely asked for a squadron of men at arms, ready to fire a salvo and that was brought for them. [...] Afterwards they took a deep bow and said: we will see each other next year and then they collapsed. When they came to they were greatly fatigued and the wretches did not remember a single thing. Finding themselves in the midst of such a multitude of people they only begged to be taken home. (*Lettere memorabilia istorche, politiche ed erudite* 141ff)

We get another firsthand account of the tarantic cure in action from Ludovico Valletta:

> The families of the *tarantati* hire the musicians, to whom many gifts are given and a great deal of drink is offered in addition to the daily compensation agreed upon, so that they may take some refreshment and thus play the musical instruments with greater vigor. It follows that a man of modest conditions, who laboriously earns a living with the diligent fatigue of his arms, in order to be cured of this illness, is often forced to pawn or sell objects of fundamental necessity, even if his household furnishings are shabby, in order to pay the aforementioned payment. It must be considered that no one would want to expose himself to this misfortune if he could combat the poison in another way, or if he did not feel compelled to dance from the bottom of his heart. I will spare the details of the many other aids and expedients the poison victims use to raise and cheer their melancholy spirits during the dance, items also needed for one reason or another. For instance there are artificial springs of limpid water constructed in such a way that the water is gathered and always returns to flow anew; these springs are covered and surrounded by green fronds, flowers and trees. Further, lasses dressed in sumptuous wedding gowns have the task of dancing with the *tarantati*, festively singing and playing the same melody with them during the dance; then there are the weapons and the multicolored drapery hung on the walls. All of these, and many others, cannot be procured without payment. (*De Phalangio Apulo* 92)

Which is noteworthy for its strong parallels to a Bacchic rite carried out by Marcus Antonius for which he imported musicians from Italy, as recorded by Sokrates the Rhodian:

> Antony himself, when he was staying at Athens, a short time after this, prepared a very superb scaffold to spread over the theatre,

covered with green wood such as is seen in the caves sacred to Bacchus; and from this scaffold he suspended drums and fawn-skins, and all the other toys which one names in connection with Bacchus, and then sat there with his friends, getting drunk from daybreak, a band of musicians, whom he had sent for from Italy, playing to him all the time, and all the Greeks around being collected to see the sight. And presently, he crossed over to the Acropolis, the whole city of Athens being illuminated with lamps suspended from the roof; and after that lie ordered himself to be proclaimed as Bacchus throughout all the cities in that district. (*History of the Civil War* Book 3 quoted in Athenaios 4.29)

The Dionysian parallels do not cease there. As R. continues:

De Martino interprets tarantism primarily as a form of psychological therapy. For him, the Tarantella is an exorcism, as a ritual eviction of the spider which possesses the victim. The spider symbolises a traumatic event in the biography of the victim (specifically frustrated eros), and it is the memory of that traumatic effect which causes the affliction of tarantism with its attendant symptoms. This memory is cast out by music, colour and dance – the tarantella. For De Martino, the symbol of the taranta is a "mythical-ritual horizon of evocation, release and resolution of unresolved psychic conflicts (…). As a cultural model, the symbol offers a mythical-ritual order for settling these conflicts and reintegrating individuals into the group. The symbol of the taranta lends a figure to the formless, rhythm and melody to menacing silence, and colour to the colourless in an assiduous quest of articulated and distinct passions, where a horizonless excitation alternates with a depression that isolates and closes off."

Gilbert Rouget, however, interpreted the phenomenon differently:

Despite appearances, the divinity responsible for the possession is not the one that is excorcised. On the contrary, it is the divinity concerned who, by allowing the possessing person to identify with him or her, provides the means of exorcising the illness – real or imagined – from which the person is suffering. (*Music and Trance: a theory of the relations between music and possession*)

Mediating against the agonistic interpretation of tarantism are the songs used by the afflicted to invoke their saintly spider:

> *Santu Paulu miu de le tarante*
> *Pizzichi le caruse a mmienzu all' anche*
> *Santu Paulu miu de li scursuni*
> *Pizzichi li carusi a li cujuni*
>
> (My St. Paul of the *tarantate*
> who pricks the girls in their genitals,
> my St. Paul of the serpents
> who pricks the boys in their testicles)

As well as:

> *Santu Paulu veni mo'*
> *Santu Paulu veni qua*
> *Tene ferme le mie catene*
> *Ma nu abbandunare.*
>
> (Saint Paul come to me,
> come here,
> hold tightly my chains,
> do not leave me.)

And:

> *Santu Paulu resta qua*
> *Nella mia casetta insieme imu restar . . .*
> *Santu Paulu veni qua*
> *Cu la manu benedetta mi devi de sanar*
> *Santu Paulu veni qua*
> *E damme la mia vita ca ieu te deu lu cor!*
> *Santu Paulu veni qua cerca la Caterina e nu me abbandunar!*
>
> (St. Paul stay here,
> in my little house stay with me . . .
> St. Paul give me the cure with your healing hand.
> St. Paul come here
> and give me my life as I give you my heart.
> St Paul come here, look for Caterina and never leave me.)

Which has led Andromache Karanika to observe:

> The character is intensely erotic. It is, then, only legitimate to see that earlier cults, pagan in origin, have been accommodated within the local Christian cults. The erotic frame is clearly noted in all the

songs used by the *tarantati/e*. In some songs it tends to be more graphic while in others the intense religious voice is equated with the passion of the devoted to the saint.

These simple songs form an intense prayer. The women seek appropriation of the saint to whom the desired cure is directed. The content of their songs justifies the name given by the locals to these women, which is precisely how they see themselves, as *spose di San Paolo* (brides of St. Paul). The dance performance reveals a latent sexual content as it follows the progress of a wedding ceremony.

Intense preparation is followed by a moment of absolute self-giving to the god, and finally exhaustion after the demanding performance. The climax of the performance is not the musical part, nor the dance performance per se, it is the moment of complete giving up of one's senses, after the task of "purification" and healing has been completed. The real climax is the moment of self-rendering with a complete trust to the divine. When the *tarantato/a* lies down, he/she resembles patients in Antiquity waiting for the cure in incubation. The main difference is that the recurrence of tarantism and the social and psychological sides interwoven therein makes us wonder to what extent one really wants a cure.

It seems from most accounts that the real goal is to remain in complete union with the divine. The account of a tarantata called Maria is very revealing in this regard, and most accounts consider hers to be a representative example. She was a tormented teenager who fell in love with someone who did not return her love. One day she felt she was "bitten" by a spider and wanted helplessly to dance. The story becomes more complicated as another woman attempted to have Maria married off to her son. The proposal was not very appealing to Maria, and in her endeavor to gain time she collected money to pay for the musicians' cure. The would-be mother-in-law, together with her son, abducted Maria. After some time she claims to have seen both St. Peter and St. Paul, as she was walking, who asked her to follow them. She started wandering around the fields and danced incessantly.

Such an incident is typical of the sorts of relationships and the psychology involved in tarantism. The conception of unity with the saint alludes to the Dionysian past and the role of the maenads in religion and in everyday life. It also alludes to the relationship between mortals and gods in antiquity as it was expressed in the gods' cult.

And rightly so for this process, according to Damascius, was central to the mysteries of Dionysos:

> The titanic mode of life is the irrational mode, by which rational life is torn asunder: it is better to acknowledge its existence everywhere, since in any case at its source there are gods, the Titans; then also on the plane of rational life, this apparent self-determination, which seems to aim at belonging to itself alone and neither to the superior nor to the inferior, is wrought in us by the Titans; through it we tear asunder the Dionysos in ourselves, breaking up the natural continuity of our being and our partnership, so to speak, with the superior and inferior. While in this condition, we are Titans; but when we recover that lost unity, we become Dionysoi and we attain what can truly be called completeness. (*Commentary on the Phaedo* 1.9)

Something we find mirrored in certain forms of Gnosticism:

> People cannot see anything in the real realm unless they become it. In the realm of truth, it is not as human beings in the world, who see the sun without being the sun, and see the sky and the earth and so forth without being them. Rather, if you have seen any things there you have become those things: if you have seen the spirit, you have become the spirit; if you have seen the anointed, you have become the anointed; if you have seen the father, you will become the father. Thus here in the world, you see everything and do not see your own self. But there, you see yourself; for you shall become what you see. (*The Gospel of Philip* 61:20-35)

Paignia Kampesiguia the Puppet

Most people translate the name of this Toy as "jointed doll" or "puppet with bendable legs" but what the Orphic verse Clement cites *actually* says is παίγνια (play, game, sport) καμπεσίγυια (limb-moving).

I'm sure the translators are correct and this was just a poetic way of describing a puppet, similar to the word for marionette which was νευρόσπαστος "the thing that's drawn around by strings."

After all Dionysos was quite fond of puppets and marionettes.

Herodotos records this fact:

> The rest of the festival of Dionysos is observed by the Egyptians much as it is by the Greeks, except for the dances; but in place of the phallos, they have invented the use of puppets two feet high and moved by strings, the male member nodding and nearly as big as the rest of the body, which are carried about the villages by women; a flute-player goes ahead, the women follow behind singing of Dionysos. Why the male member is so large and is the only part of the body that moves, there is a sacred legend that explains. (Herodotos, *The Histories* 2.48)

As does Lucian:

> I approve of the remarks about the temple made by those who in the main accept the theories of the Greeks: according to these the goddess is Hera, but the work was carried out by Dionysos, the son of Semele: Dionysos visited Syria on his journey to Aethiopia. There are in the temple many tokens that Dionysos was its actual founder:

> for instance, barbaric raiment, Indian precious stones, and elephants' tusks brought by Dionysos from the Aethiopians. Further, a pair of phalli of great size are seen standing in the vestibule, bearing the inscription, 'I, Dionysos, dedicated these phalli to Hera my stepmother.' This proof satisfies me. And I will describe another curiosity to be found in this temple, a sacred symbol of Dionysos. The Greeks erect phalli in honour of Dionysos, and on these they carry, singular to say, mannikins made of wood, with enormous pudenda; they call these puppets. There is this further curiosity in the temple: as you enter, on the right hand, a small brazen statue meets your eye of a man in a sitting posture, with parts of monstrous size. (*De Dea Syria* 15-16)

And Heron of Alexandria recorded the use of automata in a Bacchic temple in his *Peri Automatopoietikes*:

> The movable case shows, at its upper part, a platform from which arises a cylindrical temple, the roof of which, supported by six columns, is conical and surmounted by a figure of Victory with spread wings and holding a crown in her right hand. In the center of the temple Bacchus is seen standing, holding a thyrsus in his left hand, and a cup in his right. At his feet lies a panther. In front of and behind the god, on the platform of the stage, are two altars provided with combustible material. Very near the columns, but external to them, there are bacchantes placed in any posture that may be desired. All being thus prepared, the automatic apparatus is set in motion. The theater then moves of itself to the spot selected, and there stops. Then the altar in front of Bacchus becomes lighted, and, at the same time, milk and water spurt from his thyrsus, while his cup pours wine over the panther. The four faces of the base become encircled with crowns, and, to the noise of drums and cymbals, the bacchantes dance round about the temple. Soon, the noise having ceased, Victory on the top of the temple, and Bacchus within it, face about. The altar that was behind the god is now in front of him, and becomes lighted in its turn. Then occurs another outflow from the thyrsus and cup, and another round of the bacchantes to the sound of drums and cymbals. The dance being finished, the theater returns to its former station. Thus ends the apotheosis.

But calling it παίγνια καμπεσίγυια puts an interesting emphasis not on the object – as you'd expect in a list of items the savage ancestral spirits have set out as bait for the curious young god – but rather on the process of bringing that object to life:

> Puppet theatre is a highly refined art, but depends on something like a child's, a clown's, or a mad person's relation to objects. They are dead things that belong to a different kind of life. (Kenneth Gross, *Puppet: An Essay on Uncanny Life*)

Which naturally reminds one of the "limb-bending game" that Oppian describes in the *Cynegetica*:

> And, when Dionysos was now come to boyhood, he played with the other children; he would cut a fennel stalk and smite the hard rocks, and from their wounds they poured for the god sweet liquor. Otherwhiles he rent rams, skins and all, and clove them piecemeal and cast the dead bodies on the ground; and again with his hands he neatly put their limbs together, and immediately they were alive and browsed on the green pasture.

Kenneth Gross goes on to say:

> At times, the puppet shares with the mask a power to give form to gods and demons, to the spirits of the dead. In such cases the manipulator, even the puppet itself, can take on the guise of a priest or shaman.

Dionysian *mania* can involve both an ecstatic stepping out of one's self and *enthousiasmos*, being filled with the spirit of a god, as Euripides shows in the *Trachinian Women*:

> I am raised up and I will not reject the flute,
> O ruler of my mind. Look, he stirs me up,
> Euhoi, the ivy now whirls me round in Bacchic contest.

And Plato in the *Ion*:

> For all good poets, epic as well as lyric, compose their beautiful poems not by art, but because they are inspired and possessed. And as the Corybantic revellers when they dance are not in their right mind, so the lyric poets are not in their right mind when they are composing their beautiful strains: but when falling under the power of music and metre they are inspired and possessed; like Bacchic maidens who draw milk and honey from the rivers when they are under the influence of Dionysos but not when they are in their right mind. And the soul of the lyric poet does the same, as they themselves say; for they tell us that they bring songs from honeyed fountains, culling them out of the gardens and dells of the Muses;

they, like the bees, winging their way from flower to flower. And this is true. For the poet is a light and winged and holy thing, and there is no invention in him until he has been inspired and is out of his senses, and the mind is no longer in him: when he has not attained to this state, he is powerless and is unable to utter his oracles. (533e-534b)

Philo specifically compares this state to ventriloquism:

For generally the prophet proclaims nothing on his own. Rather, he merely lends his voice to him who prompts everything that he says. When he is inspired he becomes unconscious. Thought fades away and leaves the fortress of the soul. But the divine Spirit has entered there and made its dwelling. And it makes all the vocal organs sound, so that the man expresses clearly what the Spirit gives him to say. (*On The Special Laws* 4.3)

Which hearkens back to accounts of Eurykles:

Ventriloquist: belly-prophet (*engastrimantis*). Some people now call this a Python; Sophokles uses the word chest-prophet (*sternomantis*) and Plato the philosopher Eurykles after a prophet by this name. Philochoros in the third book of his *On Divination* says that women too are ventriloquists. These called up the souls of the dead. Saul used one of them, who called up the soul of Samuel. (Suidas s.v. *engastrimuthos*)

Eurykles was a prophet who manifested himself through others. So he says, "In imitation of the prophetic method of Eurykles, he entered their stomachs and poured out lots of comedy." (Scholiast on Aristophanes' *Wasps* 1015-22)

Comedy, like tragedy, is thought to have evolved out of early agrarian rites performed in honor of Dionysos. Dionysos, in addition to being the god of actors, is also the god of vegetation – and especially of the vintage. His spirit dwells in the grape on the vine. Therefore when the vintners harvested the crop, plucking the ripe fruit and then stomping the grapes and pressing them to make wine, they were, in fact, enacting a savage rite whereby the god was murdered and dismembered. At the end of the harvest men would smear their faces with the lees and sing a mournful dirge in his memory to placate his spirit and ensure that the god was not vengeful since he lived on in the drink made from his flesh. This disguise – either to hide their true identities or to give expression to the feeling of intoxicating *enthousiasmos* brought on by the consumption of alcohol, with the god's spirit rising up within them and taking hold of their bodies, making them move and speak in ways they never would otherwise – grew more elaborate until men began fashioning intricate masks out of the different kinds of wood sacred to him. At the same time the harvest-songs became more formal, with choruses of men singing and dancing and miming incidents from the life and death of the god.

> As to the rites of Dionysos, you know, without my telling you, that they consisted in dancing from beginning to end. Of the three main types of dance, the *cordax*, the *sicinnis*, and the *emmelia*, each was the invention and bore the name of one of the Satyrs, his followers. Assisted by this art, and accompanied by these revellers, he conquered Tyrrhenians, Indians, Lydians, dancing those warlike tribes into submission. [...] The Bacchic form of pantomime, which is particularly popular in Ionia and Pontus, in spite of its being confined to satyric subjects has taken such possession of those peoples, that when the pantomime season comes round in each city they leave all else and sit for whole days watching Titans and Corybantes, Satyrs and neat-herds. Men of the highest rank and position are not ashamed to take part in these performances: indeed, they pride themselves more on their pantomimic skill than on birth and ancestry and public services. (Lucian, *On the Dance*)

Out of this eventually arose the art of drama, with the performances no longer just about the sufferings and triumphs of Dionysos. In time the actor came to impersonate other figures such as famous kings and heroes who had endured similar torments and transformations. By the time that the triad of great Athenian playwrights – Aischylos, Sophokles, and Euripides – came on the scene, much about the art-form had changed, and under their skilled hands it would undergo even greater transformation. These men and their lesser-known contemporaries were responsible for introducing more roles so that it was no longer just a single actor accompanied by a chorus up on the stage. They also broadened the themes of tragedy so that they could tell a much wider assortment of stories. They brought in props and mechanical devices – including a contraption of levers and pulleys whereby an actor could be lowered down from on high at a pivotal moment in the plot (usually an improbable rescue of the seemingly doomed hero – the famous *deus ex machina*). Some conservatives resented these innovations, giving rise to the tag "What has this to do with Dionysos?" which was used especially when they did not care for a play.

No matter how much it changed, however, *mimesis* remained a central component of the dramatic arts.

According to Mike Mowbray:

The 'mimetic faculty' is an elusive concept, foregrounding a human inclination to mimic or to imitate, to produce symbolic forms, representations and artefacts that mirror and also perhaps transform their objects. In essence, the notion may be described as referring to a capacity to produce and to recognize similarity. Although it is difficult to identify any essential origin or core that is preeminent and enduring in the cultural and intellectual history of the concept, it is possible to reach back to Greek antiquity for a pre-platonic root of the term mimesis. The term, derived from the word 'mimos', meaning mime or mimic, then (as now) revolved around questions of imitation, representation, and expression. The root term makes some of its earliest recorded appearances, for example in the Delian hymn or in a fragment from the philosopher Aeschylus (c. 525-456BC), in the context of music and dance – prompting some scholars to fix an early meaning in reference to acts of representation through dance. This view is disputed, however, as others refuse such a narrow definition, even in this early context (Gebauer and Wulf 1995: 6, 25-30). Gerald Else, for example, suggests three possible implications associated with the term 'mimesis': (1) 'Miming': direct representation of the looks, actions and/or utterances of animals or men through speech, song or dancing. (2) 'Imitation' of the actions of one person by another, in a general sense. (3) 'Replication': an image or effigy of a person or thing in material form. Mimos, or mimesis, may be said to generate impure, adulterated, or creatively inflected representations, or imitations, which exaggerate or project qualities that are nonetheless essentially similar between the object and its representation through mimetic endeavour. Such a view finds echoes in Aristotle, who concerned himself mainly with mimesis' role in image-production and literary creation. For Aristotle, such processes have a tendency to simultaneously produce the possible and the general, to give rise to the literary fable or plot, to render their objects as fiction (as adulterated or creatively-inflected representation) in which only a mediated reference to 'objective' reality persists. In so doing, mimesis is a "process of re-creation," which introduces "embellishment, improvement and the generalization of individual qualities" (ibid: 26). In contradistinction to Plato's concern that mimetic endeavors pose a danger of giving rise to a world of appearances or illusory images, which could erode adherence to the strictly conceptual models (or Ideas) that he saw as a preferred basis for social ordering and education, the view which arises in Aristotle appears to give license to the positive and creative potentiality of a human capacity for mimesis.

Antonin Artaud felt Plato's concerns about *mimesis* were entirely justified, going so far as to compare theater to the plague:

> For if theatre is like the plague, this is not just because it acts on large groups and disturbs them in one and the same way. There is both something victorious and vengeful in theatre just as in the plague, for we clearly feel that the spontaneous fire the plague lights as it passes by is nothing but a gigantic liquidation. The plague takes dormant images, latent disorder and suddenly carries them to the point of the most extreme gestures. Theatre also takes gestures and develops them to the limit. Just like the plague, it reforges the links between what does and does not exist, between the virtual nature of the possible and the material nature of existence. It rediscovers the idea of figures and archetypal symbols which act like sudden silences, fermatas, heart stops, adrenalin calls, incendiary images surging into our abruptly woken minds. It restores all our dormant conflicts and their powers, giving these powers names we acknowledge as signs. Here a bitter clash of symbols takes place before us, hurled one against the other in an inconceivable riot. For theatre can only happen the moment the inconceivable really begins, where poetry taking place on stage nourishes and superheats created symbols. These symbols are symbols of full-blown powers held in bondage until that moment and unusable in real life, exploding in the guise of incredible images giving existence and the freedom of the city to acts naturally opposed to social life. A real stage play disturbs our peace of mind, releases our repressed subconscious, drives us to a kind of potential rebellion (since it retains its full value only if it remains potential), calling for a difficult heroic attitude on the part of the assembled groups.

And in fact, such theatrical epidemics are known to have occurred:

> There is a story of a curious epidemic at Abdera, just after the accession of King Lysimachus. It began with the whole population's exhibiting feverish symptoms, strongly marked and consistent from the very first attack. About the seventh day, the fever was relieved, in some cases by a violent flow of blood from the nose, in others by perspiration no less violent. The mental effects, however, were most ridiculous; they were all stage-struck, mouthing blank verse and ranting at the top of their voices. Their favourite recitation was the *Andromeda* of Euripides; one after another would go through the great speech of Perseus; the whole place was full of pale ghosts, who were our seventh-day tragedians vociferating: 'O Love, who lord'st

it over gods and men...' and the rest of it. This continued for some time, till the coming of winter put an end to their madness with a sharp frost. I find the explanation of the form the madness took in this fact: Archelaus was then the great tragic actor, and in the middle of the summer, during some very hot weather, he had played the *Andromeda* in Abdera; most of them took the fever in the theatre, and convalescence was followed by a relapse – into tragedy, the *Andromeda* haunting their memories. (Lucian, *How to Write History*)

Which calls to mind epidemics of a different sort which were behind the festivals of the Dionysian heroines Erigone:

Icarius' dog returned to his daughter, Erigone; she followed his tracks and, when she found her father's corpse, she ended her life with a noose. Through the mercy of the gods she was restored to life again among the constellations; men call her Virgo. That dog was also placed among the stars. But after some time such a sickness was sent upon the Athenians that their maidens were driven by a certain madness to hang themselves. The oracle responded that this pestilence could be stopped if the corpses of Erigone and Icarius were sought again. These were found nowhere after being sought for a long time. Then, to show their devotedness, and to appear to seek them in another element, the Athenians hung rope from trees. Holding on to this rope, the men were tossed here and there so that they seemed to seek the corpses in the air. But since most were falling from the trees, they decided to make shapes in the likeness of their own faces and hang these in place of themselves. Hence, little masks are called *oscilla* because in them faces oscillate, that is, move. (*The First Vatican Mythographer* 19)

And Charilla:

The Delphians celebrate three festivals one after the other which occur every eight years, the first of which they call Septerion, the second Heroïs, and the third Charilla. The greater part of the Heroïs has a secret import which the Thyiads know; but from the portions of the rites that are performed in public one might conjecture that it represents the evocation of Semele. The story of Charilla which they relate is somewhat as follows: A famine following a drought oppressed the Delphians, and they came to the palace of their king with their wives and children and made supplication. The king gave portions of barley and legumes to the more notable citizens, for there was not enough for all. But when an orphaned girl, who was still but a small child, approached him and importuned him, he struck her with his sandal and cast the sandal in her face. But, although the girl was poverty-stricken and without protectors, she was not ignoble in character; and when she had withdrawn, she took off her girdle and hanged herself. As the famine increased and diseases also were added thereto, the prophetic priestess gave an oracle to the king that he must appease Charilla, the maiden who had slain herself. Accordingly, when they had discovered with some difficulty that this was the name of the child who had been struck, they performed a certain sacrificial rite combined with purification, which even now they continue to perform every eight years. For the king sits in state and gives a portion of barley-meal and legumes to everyone, alien and citizen alike, and a doll-like image of Charilla is brought thither. When, accordingly, all have received a portion, the king strikes the image with his sandal. The leader of the Thyiads picks up the image and bears it to a certain place which is full of chasms; there they tie a rope round the neck of the image and bury it in the place where they buried Charilla after she had hanged herself. (Plutarch, *Aetia Graeca* 12)

Note the presence of dolls and masks in these myths of epidemic.

Another level of this is explored in Michael Turner's *The Woman in White: Dionysos and the dance of death*:

> The 'woman in white' is in the process of reversing the ecstatic process. She is, as it were, stepping out of her marble dead body and back into the one of flesh and blood she had prior to death; note the colour of her black hair. Her powers of motion, sight, and speech are returning. She has stepped off her base and is dancing ecstatically, beating a drum, as she returns to life – albeit a life eternally confined to the afterlife. Once the process is complete her flesh, as on the other two women on the krater, will have returned to its natural pre-death colour. It is the Sydney krater that gives us the clue to understanding this and similar imagery.
>
> Similar imagery appears on an unprovenanced bell-krater now in Oxford, where a woman playing the aulos steps off a two-tiered platform. Although red-coloured, she is white-skinned. The platform too is red. Four youths surround her, all wreathed, and with one arm raised as if in greeting. Like the satyr on the Nicholson krater, the figure to her immediate right is bending down as if to help her off the platform. To his right, a youth advances holding out a tray or basket. To the left, both figures carry lit torches suggesting a setting away from the daylight.

[...]
The petrification of Niobe is unknown in Attic art. It first appears at the beginning of the 4th century BC, with the earliest extant example a fragmentary South Italian amphora from grave 24 at Roccagloriosa in Campania. Niobe is shown slowly turning to stone, standing on a high base. The effect is achieved by portraying her bottom half as a white block. The imagery is subsequently developed on both Campanian and Apulian pottery with the dying woman shown standing inside a naiskos.

[...]
The woman is youthful. Her imagery and that of similar Dionysiac figures, both male and female, is always youthful. As such, it parallels contemporary funerary statuary where deceased old age and the ravages of time and disease are never shown. This is the representation of idealized eternal youth – the dead both as they would like to have been remembered, and as those who remained wanted to remember them, *panta kala*, when everything was beautiful. It is the perception of (after)life as it will be, not of mortal life as it was.

Despite the very youthful imagery of Dionysiac initiates on pottery, the reality would appear to have been very different. The god made no distinction amongst his worshippers as to age or sex (Euripides, *Bacchae* 206-10). Both Euripides and Aristophanes describe the participation of older people, both male and female. In the *Frogs* (341-9), the chorus of initiates, young and old, male and female, describes the liberating effects of ecstatic Dionysiac dance for elderly initiates. In the *Bacchae*, despite their age the elderly Cadmus and Teiresias put on fawn skins and ivy wreaths and holding thyrsi prepare to join the *thiasos* (176-7). Both men say that dancing ecstatically makes them forget their age and feel young again, and physically enables them to dance tirelessly, despite their lameness (187-90).

Beneath the figured scenes is a meander pattern. Some bell-kraters, the Paestan kraters for example, have wave patterns. It should perhaps now be asked why these are the only two designs seen as apotropaic decoration on kraters of this type, whether Attic or South Italian.

The meander is the figure of a labyrinth in linear form. Kerényi suggests that we should set aside our concept of a labyrinth as a place in which one can lose one's way, arguing instead that 'it is a confusing path, hard to follow without a thread, but provided one is not devoured at the mid-point, it leads surely, despite twists and turns, back to the beginning. Safely negotiated, it will lead to salvation, or within the iconological context of this pottery, to an afterlife.'

The wave pattern recalls the alternative journey across the sea to the afterlife. J.-P. Descoeudres, in relation to similar imagery in Etruscan funerary wall-painting, suggests that it represents the boundary that must be crossed to get from the world of the living (i.e. the viewer) to the world of the dead, represented by imagery above the waves.

Pókos the Tuft of Wool

Clement is our only author to include Pókos among the Toys, though as we saw earlier Epiphanios listed "worked wool" among the contents of the *kiste* or basket of the mysteries. Although usage is not consistent, πόκος is a word with ancient pedigree (found as far back as Homer's *Iliad* 12.451) for fleece or wool in its raw, recently sheared state. In fact the forms πέκω and πόκες were used analogously of harvesting and separation, providing an indication of one of this Toy's primary functions. Appropriately the word λῆνος, also meaning wool or fleece, but most often wool that has been carded and prepared for weaving, gives us an opposite but equally important indication.

Within a Hellenic context, mention of fleece almost certainly calls to mind Jason and the heroic Argonauts' quest for the golden fleece of Phrixos. The legends associated with this are significant within the Starry Bull tradition for a number of reasons. Two of its most important heroes, Orpheus and Herakles, were among the crew of the Argo – not to mention Philasos and Eurymedon (*Hyginus, Fabulae 14*) as well as Phanos and Staphylos (Apollodoros, *Bibliotheca 1.113*), all four of whom were sons of Dionysos and Ariadne. During their travels through the Black Sea region these sailor-adventurers met Ariadne's cousin Medeia (*Apollonios Rhodios, Argonautika 3.1074*) who taught Orpheus the use of drugs and *epodai* or magical songs to raise the dead, according to the late *Orphic Argonautika*.

They also traced the footsteps of Asterios the Minotaur:

> Asterios conceived a bastard passion for the strange country, being hard of heart. He was not again to see his native land and the cave

of the Idaian mount shimmering with helmets; he preferred a life of exile, and instead of Dikte he became a Knossian settler in Skythia. He left greyheaded Minos and his wife; the civilized one joined the barbaric tribes of guest-murdering Colchians, called them Asterians, they whose nature provided them with outlandish customs. (Nonnos, *Dionysiaka* 13.238-252)

This is also the area in which king Skyles suffered martyrdom through decapitation (like Orpheus, Lykourgos and Pentheus) by his people for participating in Dionysian *teletai*:

So when Skyles had been initiated into the Bacchic rite, some one of the Borysthenites scoffed at the Skythians, 'You laugh at us, Skythians, because we play the Bacchant and the god possesses us; but now this deity has possessed your own king, so that he plays the Bacchant and is maddened by the god. If you will not believe me, follow me now and I will show him to you.' The leading men among the Skythians followed him, and the Borysthenite brought them up secretly onto a tower; from which, when Skyles passed by with his company of worshipers, they saw him raving like a Bacchant; thinking it a great misfortune, they left the city and told the whole army what they had seen. After this Skyles rode off to his own place; but the Skythians rebelled against him [...]Oktamasadas beheaded Skyles upon the spot. Thus rigidly do the Skythians maintain their own customs, and thus severely do they punish such as adopt foreign usages. (Herodotos, *Histories* 4.79)

And where the Greek settlement of Olbia was established, home of some of the earliest archaeological evidence for Bacchic Orphic cults to come down to us. Most people are familiar with the enigmatic bone tablets I cited earlier, but there is also a ritual mirror most likely belonging to a woman who engaged in maenadic rites, bearing the inscription "Demonassa, daughter of Lenaios, euai!" (*SEG* 143.92) This is the first recorded instance of the famous Bacchic cry, which will be echoed in a Sibylline oracle given to a neighboring population:

Greetings! Oracle of the Sibyl: "When Bakchos, after having shouted euai, is struck, then blood, fire, and ash will be united." Set up by Spellios Euethis, *archiboukolos*, Herakleides son of Alexandros being *archimystos*, Alexandros being *speirarchos*. (*IPerinthos* 57)

The golden fleece has an even more direct Dionysian connection, however:

> Of the sons of Aeolus, Athamas ruled over Boeotia and begat a son Phrixos and a daughter Helle by Nephele. And he married a second wife, Ino, by whom he had Learchos and Melikertes. But Ino plotted against the children of Nephele and persuaded the women to parch the wheat; and having got the wheat they did so without the knowledge of the men. But the earth, being sown with parched wheat, did not yield its annual crops; so Athamas sent to Delphi to inquire how he might be delivered from the dearth. Now Ino persuaded the messengers to say it was foretold that the infertility would cease if Phrixos were sacrificed to Zeus. When Athamas heard that, he was forced by the inhabitants of the land to bring Phrixos to the altar. But Nephele caught him and her daughter up and gave them a ram with a golden fleece, which she had received from Hermes, and borne through the sky by the ram they crossed land and sea. But when they were over the sea which lies betwixt Sigeum and the Chersonese, Helle slipped into the deep and was drowned, and the sea was called Hellespont after her. But Phrixos came to the Colchians, whose king was Aeetes, son of the Sun and of Perseis, and brother of Circe and Pasiphae, whom Minos married. He received Phrixos and gave him one of his daughters, Chalkiope. And Phrixos sacrificed the ram with the golden fleece to Zeus the God of Escape, and the fleece he gave to Aeetes, who nailed it to an oak in a grove of Ares. And Phrixos had children by Chalkiope, to wit, Argos, Melas, Phrontis, and Kytisoros. (Apollodoros, *Bibliotheca* 1.9.1)

Semele's sister, doomed children, and a drowning maiden all feature prominently in the myth of Dionysos' fosterage:

> At the proper time Zeus loosened the stitches and gave birth to Dionysos, whom he entrusted to Hermes. Hermes took him to Ino and Athamas, and persuaded them to bring him up as a girl. Incensed, Hera inflicted madness on them, so that Athamas stalked and slew his elder son Learchos on the conviction that he was a deer, while Ino threw Melikertes into a basin of boiling water, and then, carrying both the basin and the corpse of the boy, she jumped to the bottom of the sea. Now she is called Leukothea, and her son is Palaimon: these names they receive from those who sail, for they help sailors beset by storms. Also, the Isthmian games were established by Sisyphos in honor of Melikertes. (ibid 3.26-29)

Melikertes' immersion and subsequent *apotheosis*, as well as Helle's ram, should call to mind this passage from the Bacchic Orphic gold leaf from Thurii:

And I plunged down into the lap of my lady, the subterranean queen.
'Happy and fortunate one, you will be a god from the mortal you were.'
A ram, I fell into the milk.

This was not the only instance where Hera's mad rage rent the happy existence of the young god, as Olympiodoros reminds us in his commentary on the *Phaido* of Plato:

> The form of that which is universal is plucked off, torn in pieces, and scattered into generation; and Dionysos is the *monad* of the Titans. But his laceration is said to take place through the stratagems of Hera, because this goddess is the supervising guardian of motion and progression; and on this account, in the *Iliad*, she perpetually rouses and excites Zeus to providential action about secondary concerns; and, in another respect, Dionysos is the *ephorus* or supervising guardian of generation, because he presides over life and death; for he is the guardian or *ephorus* of life because of generation, and also of death because wine produces an enthusiastic condition. We become more enthusiastic at the period of dying, as Proclus indicates in the example of Homer who became prophetic at the time of his death. They likewise assert that tragedy and comedy are assigned to Dionysos: comedy being the play or ludicrous representation of life; and tragedy having relation to the passions and death. The comic writers, therefore, do not rightly call in question the tragedians as not rightly representing Dionysos, saying that such things did not happen to Dionysos. But Zeus is said to have hurled his thunder at the Titans; the thunder signifying a conversion or changing: for fire naturally ascends; and hence Zeus, by this means, converts the Titans to his own essence.

An anonymous commentator of Clement's also links the dismemberment of Dionysos, dramatic arts and wool, albeit indirectly:

> *Lenaizontas* – a rustic song sung at the wine trough, which even itself has to do with the dismemberment of Dionysos. Clement has put very well and gracefully the bit about "binding up with ivy", at the same time showing the fact that the Lenaian festivals are dedicated to Dionysos and also how as drunken mischief these things have been clapped together by tipsy and drunken people. (Scholiast to *Protrepticus* 1.2.2 p. 297.4)

For he perpetuates the misnomer that the festival Λήναια and those who celebrate it, the Λῆναι, derive their name from ληνός (wine-press) when it much more likely comes from λῆνος (wool). Not only does the accentuation fall in the wrong place for that derivation to work, but more importantly, none of our sources – visual or literary – show any involvement of the wine-press in this festival. It would be pretty astounding if they did since Lenaia fell during the middle of winter and for the most part within our January. Should one leave behind the ivory walls of academia they would be hard pressed to find grapes still on the vine or being crushed at this time of year in Greece or anywhere else for that matter. There were only a few weeks left at this point until the casks were broached and the new wine tasted for the first time at Anthesteria. All the hard work had already been done months before, around the time of Oschophoria and the other autumn harvest festivals:

> At the festival of the Oschophoria it is not the herald that is crowned, but his herald's staff, and those who are present at the libations cry out: "Eleleu! Iou! Iou!" the first of which cries is the exclamation of eager haste and triumph, the second of consternation and confusion. It was Theseus who instituted the Athenian festival of the Oschophoria. For it is said that he did not take away with him all the maidens on whom the lot fell at that time, but picked out two young men of his acquaintance who had fresh and girlish faces, but eager and manly spirits, and changed their outward appearance almost entirely by giving them warm baths and keeping them out of the sun, by arranging their hair, and by smoothing their skin and beautifying their complexions with unguents; he also taught them to imitate maidens as closely as possible in their speech, their dress, and their gait, and to leave no difference that could be observed, and then enrolled them among the maidens who were going to Crete, and was undiscovered by any. And when he was come back, he himself and these two young men headed a procession, arrayed as those are now arrayed who carry the vine-branches. They carry these in honour of Dionysos and Ariadne, and because of their part in the story; or rather, because they came back home at the time of the vintage. And the women called Deipnophoroi, or supper-carriers, take part in the procession and share in the sacrifice, in imitation of the mothers of the young men and maidens on whom the lot fell, for these kept coming with bread and meat for their children. And tales are told at this festival, because these mothers, for the sake of comforting and encouraging their children, spun out tales for them. At that feast they also carry the so-called *eiresione*, which is a bough of olive wreathed with wool, such as Theseus used at the time of his supplication, and laden with all sorts of fruit-

offerings, to signify that scarcity was at an end, and as they go they sing:—

> Eiresione for us brings figs and bread of the richest,
> Brings us honey in pots and oil to rub off from the body,
> Strong wine too in a beaker, that one may go to bed mellow.

(Demon, fragment of *Atthis* as preserved in Plutarch's *Life of Theseus*)

Of course, one needn't even leave those ivory walls to determine that Lenaia is not the festival when the wine was pressed, for Hesiod remarks of the month in which it falls:

> Avoid the month Lenaeon, wretched days, all of them fit to skin an ox, and the frosts which are cruel when Boreas blows over the earth. He blows across horse-breeding Thrace upon the wide sea and stirs it up, while earth and the forest howl. On many a high-leafed oak and thick pine he falls and brings them to the bounteous earth in mountain glens: then all the immense wood roars and the beasts shudder and put their tails between their legs, even those whose hide is covered with fur; for with his bitter blast he blows even through them, although they are shaggy-breasted. He goes even through an ox's hide; it does not stop him. Also he blows through the goat's fine hair. But through the fleeces of sheep, because their wool is abundant, the keen wind Boreas pierces not at all; but it makes the old man curved as a wheel. And it does not blow through the tender maiden who stays indoors with her dear mother, unlearned as yet in the works of golden Aphrodite, and who washes her soft body and anoints herself with oil and lies down in an inner room within the house, on a winter's day when the Boneless One gnaws his foot in his fireless house and wretched home; for the sun shows him no pastures to make for, but goes to and fro over the land and city of dusky men, and shines more sluggishly upon the whole race of the Hellenes. Then the horned and unhorned denizens of the wood, with teeth chattering pitifully, flee through the copses and glades, and all, as they seek shelter, have this one care, to gain thick coverts or some hollow rock. Then, like the Three-legged One whose back is broken and whose head looks down upon the ground, like him, I say, they wander to escape the white snow. (*Works and Days* 504-535)

Note that Hesiod specifically mentions wool in this context, as well as the skinning of an ox.

Interestingly, wool and weaving are also prominent themes in the play *Lysistrata*, which Aristophanes debuted during Lenaia:

> Women will untangle the mess of the state that men have made, just as they untangle threads while weaving. This way and that still the spool we keep passing, till it is finally clear. So to untangle the War and its errors, ambassadors out on all sides we will send. This way and that, here, there and round about–soon you will find that the War has an end. Well, first as we wash dirty wool so's to cleanse it, so with a pitiless zeal we will scrub through the whole city for all greasy fellows; burrs too, the parasites, off we will rub. That verminous plague of insensate place-seekers soon between thumb and forefinger we'll crack. All who inside Athens' walls have their dwelling into one great common basket we'll pack. Disenfranchised or citizens, allies or aliens, pell-mell the lot of them in we will squeeze. Till they discover humanity's meaning.... As for disjointed and far colonies, them you must never from this time imagine as scattered about just like lost hanks of wool. Each portion we'll take and wind in to this centre, inward to Athens each loyalty pull, till from the vast heap where all's piled together at last can be woven a strong Cloak of State.

During this civic festival at Athens Dionysos was invoked in his role as bringer of wealth and the blessings of civilization. According to Stephanus of Byzantium (s.v. *Lenaios*) the great *pompê* or procession began *en agrois* "outside the walls" or "in the countryside" and wound inward through the maze of streets until it reached his temple just beyond the marketplace. This temple was called the Lenaion and after the 5th century BCE contained one of Athens' largest theaters, capable of seating thousands (though the theater used in the City Dionysia was even bigger.) In addition to the Archon Basileos, the officials from Eleusis and local dignitaries the *pompê* consisted of actors, Dionysian priests, men in satyr costumes and women dressed as nymphs or maenads dancing with snakes. This suggests that the *pompê* was in some sense a reenactment of the triumphant army that Dionysos marched at the head of when he came to teach King Amphiktyon viticulture and how to properly mix water with wine to avoid the more dangerous side effects of the divine beverage (Athenaios 2. 38c-d). To further emphasize Dionysos' role as culture hero and founder of refined and civilizing institutions (paralleling the accomplishments of Demeter) the Daduchos or Torch-bearer of Eleusis hailed him during the sacrifice as Iakchos (the guide of initiates) and Ploutodotos (the bestower of the earth's riches) as we learn from the scholiast on Aristophanes' *Frogs* 479. Once the public sacrifice of a bull was over the dramatic contests began.

These associations were made even more explicit in the version of the festival celebrated in Ephesos and Ionia:

> The Lenaia included, according to Heraclitus' testimonium, a procession in Ephesus dedicated to the god accompanied by the hymn to the phallus, and it also records that 'Hades is the same as Dionysos, in whose honour they go mad (μαίνονται) and 'celebrate the Lenaia' or 'become *lenai*' (ληναΐζουσιν). This latter phrase provides, in our view, very valuable information about the archaic festival in Ephesus. Firstly the reference to Dionysos, identifed with Hades, indicates the god's contact with death in the festival; secondly the verb ληναΐζω may refer to the presence and importance of the women celebrating Dionysos in the festival, possibly with 'ecstatic' dancing and singing, if the verb is translated as 'becoming *lenai*' (Heraclitus uses it as a synonym for βακχεύουσι), as the scholia indicate. In fact, in another fragment, also recorded by Clement, Heraclitus alludes, amongst other groups traditionally associated with the cult of Dionysos (and the night), to the Λῆναι. The scholium ad loc. equates ληναΐζω with βακχεύουσιν, and the *lenai* with the Bacchants; and in a gloss of Hesychius the *lenai* are also equated with the Bacchants. In later literature the *lenai* are the maenads of Dionysos. Theocritus (Idyll. 26), for example, refers to the bacchants Agave, Ion and Autonoe as *lenai* or *bacchai*, and speaks of their rites at 'the 12 altars.' In a third-century BCE inscription found in Halicarnassus, Dionysos 'leads' the bacchants (θοᾶν ληναγέ – τα Βακχᾶν). The fragment of Heraclitus referred to above appears to indicate both the important part played by women who 'become Λῆναι,' at least in Ephesus in the Archaic period, and Dionysos' link with death in this ancient festival shared with the Ionians. We think that the Λῆναι had a major role in the Athenian festival awakening, invoking or calling the god from death. (Miriam Valdés Guía, *Redefining Dionysos in Athens from the Written Sources: The Lenaia, Iacchos and Attic Women*)

And notably, a *lex sacra* from nearby Miletos prescribes woolen articles to be sacrificed to Dionysos at his festival:

> ...the Prodorpia is given at the Dionysia: two stones...libations: double propitiary offerings; two stones wreathed with fillets of wool; wood. On the twelfth: at the house (?) of the Basileus the following is to be given to Dionysos: a lamp, barley, wheat groats, a pure cheese, honey, wood, flock of wool, libation: propitiary offerings, garlic, and (?); on the thirteenth: to Hera Anthea the

following is to be given: a pregnant white sheep, having mounted (to the altar) in white, a *chous* to the priestess, and wood... (*LSAM* 41)

Of course, we needn't fall into an either/or dichotomy as Thomas Taylor reminds us. Dionysos can be *both* the god of wool and the god of the winepress:

> And as to the fleece of wool, this is a symbol of laceration, or distribution of intellect, or Dionysus, into matter; for the verb σπαραττω, *sparatto, dilanio,* which is used in the relation of the Bacchic discerption, signifies to tear in pieces like wool: and hence Isidorus derives the Latin word *lana, wool,* from *laniando,* as *vellus* from *vellendo.* Nor must it pass unobserved, that λῆνος, in Greek, signifies wool, and ληνὸς, a wine-press. And, indeed, the pressing of grapes is as evident a symbol of dispersion as the tearing of wool; and this circumstance was doubtless one principal reason why grapes were consecrated to Bacchus: for a grape, previous to its pressure, aptly represents that which is collected into one; and when it is pressed into juice, it no less aptly represents the diffusion of that which was before collected and entire. (*Dissertation on the Eleusinian and Bacchic Mysteries* pgs 210-211)

This puts an interesting spin on the remainder of the passage from Hesiod I quoted above, where he was complaining about the frigidity of the month Lenaeon:

> But through the fleeces of sheep, because their wool is abundant, the keen wind Boreas pierces not at all; but it makes the old man curved as a wheel. And it does not blow through the tender maiden who stays indoors with her dear mother, unlearned as yet in the works of golden Aphrodite, and who washes her soft body and anoints herself with oil and lies down in an inner room within the house, on a winter's day when the Boneless One gnaws his foot in his fireless house and wretched home; for the sun shows him no pastures to make for, but goes to and fro over the land and city of dusky men, and shines more sluggishly upon the whole race of the Hellenes.

The virginal maiden sequestered to the loom by her mother calls to mind Kore-Persephone's condition before she was carried off by the Lord of the Underworld:

> This said, Ceres left the temple; but no speed is enough for her haste; she complains that her sluggish dragons scarce move, and,

lashing the wings now of this one and now of that (though little they deserved it), she hopes to reach Sicily e'er yet out of sight of Ida. She fears everything and hopes nothing, anxious as the bird that has entrusted its unfledged brood to a low-growing ash and while absent gathering food has many fears lest perchance the wind has blown the fragile nest from the tree, lest her young ones be exposed to the theft of man or the greed of snakes. When she saw the gate-keepers fled, the house unguarded, the rusted hinges, the overthrown doorposts, and the miserable state of the silent halls, pausing not to look again at the disaster, she rent her garment and tore away the shattered corn-ears along with her hair. She could not weep nor speak nor breathe and a trembling shook the very marrow of her bones; her faltering steps tottered. She flung open the doors and wandering through the empty rooms and deserted halls, recognized the half-ruined warp with its disordered threads and the work of the loom broken off. The goddess' labours had come to naught, and what remained to be done, that the bold spider was finishing with her sacrilegious web. (Claudian, *De Raptu Proserpine* 3.137-158)

This scene was given added significance by the Orphics:

Orpheus says that the vivific cause of partible natures, namely Persephone, while she remained on high, weaving the order of celestials, was a nymph, as being undefiled; and in consequence of this connected with Zeus and abiding in her appropriate manners; but that, proceeding from her proper habitation, she left her webs unfinished, was ravished; having been ravished, was married; and that being married, she generated in order that she might animate things which have an adventitious life. For the unfinished state of her web indicates, I think, that the universe is imperfect or unfinished, as far as to perpetual animals (i.e., the universe would be imperfect if nothing inferior to the celestial gods was produced). Hence Plato says the single creator calls on the many creators to weave together the mortal and immortal natures; after a manner reminding us, that the addition of the mortal genera is the perfection of the textorial life of the universe, and also exciting our recollection of the divine Orphic fable, and affording us interpretative causes of the unfinished webs of Persephone. (Proclus, *Commentary on Plato's Timaeus*)

More succinctly, Aristotle in his treatise *On the Generation of Animals* writes:

> In the verse ascribed to Orpheus the various organs – heart, lungs, liver, eyes, etc. – were formed successively, for he says that animals come into being in the same way as a net is woven. (734a)

The Orphics even broke it down further, assigning specific meanings to the parts of the loom:

> So what? Does not Epigenes, in his book *On the Poetry of Orpheus*, in exhibiting the peculiarities found in Orpheus, say that by "the curved rods" (κερκίσι) is meant "ploughs"; and by the warp (στήμοσι), the furrows; and the woof (μίτος) is a figurative expression for the seed; and that "tears of Zeus" signify a storm; and that the "parts" (μοῖραι) are, again, the phases of the moon, the thirtieth day, and the fifteenth, and the new moon, and that Orpheus accordingly calls them "white-robed," as being parts of the light? Again, that the Spring is called "flowery" (ἄνθιον) from its nature; and Night "still" (ἀργίς) on account of rest; and the Moon "Gorgonian," on account of the face in it; and that the time in which it is necessary to sow is called "Aphrodite" by the theologian? In the same way, too, the Pythagoreans spoke figuratively, allegorizing the "dogs of Persephone" as the planets, the "tears of Kronos" as the sea. (Clement of Alexandria, *Stromateis* 5.8.49.3)

It is not unimportant that in Claudian a spider seeks to complete Proserpine's labor, for it was the dangerous eroticism of Arachne's own weaving in Ovid's *Metamorphoses* that brought on the wrath of Minerva:

> The Maeonian girl depicts Europa deceived by the form of the bull: you would have thought it a real bull and real waves. She is seen looking back to the shore she has left, and calling to her companions, displaying fear at the touch of the surging water, and drawing up her shrinking feet. She added Jupiter who, hidden in the form of a satyr, filled Antiope, daughter of Nycteus with twin offspring; charmed Danaë as a golden shower, by the daughter of Asopus, as a flame, Mnemosyne, as a shepherd and by Proserpine, Ceres's daughter, as a spotted snake. She wove you, Neptune, also, changed to a fierce bull for Canace, Aeolus's daughter. She showed how Bacchus ensnared Erigone with delusive grapes, and how Saturn as the double of a horse begot Chiron. The outer edge of the web, surrounded by a narrow border, had flowers interwoven with entangled ivy.

Pliny went one better and attributed to her and her son all that pertained to this sacred art:

> The use of the spindle in the manufacture of woolen was invented by Closter son of Arachne, linen and nets by Arachne. (*Natural History* 7.196)

Tarentum, which lent its name to the cult of tarantism, was famed for producing the best wool in all of Italy:

> The most esteemed wool of all is that of Apulia, and that which in Italy is called Grecian wool, in other countries Italian. The fleeces of Miletus hold the third rank. The Apulian wool is shorter in the hair, and only owes its high character to the cloaks that are made of it. That which comes from the vicinity of Tarentum and Canusium is the most celebrated. (Pliny, *Natural History* 8.73)

Often this wool was used to make the famous Tarentine cloak, which was dyed scarlet-purple and contained tassels on one side, according to Hesychius. Though generally regarded as a feminine garment and a byword for luxury (Aelian, *Varia Historia* 7.9) this cloak was also part of the attire of comedic troupes in Italy, according to Athenaios (*Deipnosophistai* 14.15-16):

> And those who practiced this kind of sport were called among the Lacedæmonians δικηλισταί, which is a term equivalent to σκευοποιοί or μιμηταί. There are, however, many names, varying in different places, for this class of δικηλισταί; for the Sicyonians call them φαλλοφόροι, and others call them αὐτοκάβδαλοι, and some call them φλύακες, as the Italians do. Semos the Delian says in his book about Pæans—"The men who were called αὐτοκάβδαλοι used to wear crowns of ivy, and they would go through long poems slowly. But at a later time both they and their poems were called Iambics. And those," he proceeds, "who are called Ithyphalli, wear a mask representing the face of a drunken man, and wear crowns, having gloves embroidered with flowers. And they wear tunics shot with white; and they wear a Tarentine robe, which covers them down to their ankles: and they enter at the stage entrance silently, and when they have reached the middle of the orchestra, they turn towards the spectators, and say—
>
>> Out of the way; a clear space leave
>> For the great mighty god:
>> For the god, to his ankles clad,
>> Will pass along the centre of the crowd.
>
> And the Phallophori, says he, "wear no masks; but they put on a sort of veil of wild thyme, and on that they put acanthi, and an

untrimmed garland of violets and ivy; and they clothe themselves in Caunacæ, and so come on the stage, some at the side, and others through the centre entrance, walking in exact musical time, and saying—

> For you, O Bacchus, do we now set forth -
> This tuneful song; uttering in various melody
> This simple rhythm.
> It is a song unsuited to a virgin;
> Nor are we now addressing you with hymns
> Made long ago, but this our offering
> Is fresh unutter'd praise.

And then, advancing, they used to ridicule with their jests whoever they chose; and they did this standing still, but the Phallophoros himself marched straight on, covered with soot and dirt."

Which is perhaps why Iakchos (syncretized with the eponymous hero) was represented with a distaff on the city's coinage:

> The coins of this Molossian type are characterized by the appearance on the Tarentine dies of a peculiar and well-marked representation of Taras as a decidedly fleshy child, holding in the left hand a distaff wound round with wool. The rounded obese figure, as seen on the earliest coins of this class in some cases even verging on caricature fits on morphologically to the somewhat stumpy and heavy though maturer form of the Eponymic hero as he appears on some of the most characteristic types of the two preceding Periods.
> The motive for the intrusion of this somewhat ungainly type into the Tarentine series was, perhaps, supplied by a certain aspect of local religious cult, on which a new light has been recently thrown by the discovery of large deposits of votive terra-cotta figures, in tombs and upon the site of temples formerly contained within the walls of Tarentum. In the tombs have been found a class of abnormally fat childish figures, some of which, as, for instance, a winged genius crowned with ivy-leaves and berries, have a distinct Bacchic connexion. And the curious phase in Tarentine art-fashion attested by these figures seems, in fact, to have been associated with a deeply-rooted Tarentine cult of the Chthonic Dionysos, his consort Persephone-Kora, and their mystic progeny, the infant Iacchos, the plastic representations of whom have been found by the thousand on the site of a local sanctuary.

The kantharos of Dionysos is of frequent occurrence, and it is found, though at a slightly later date, in the hand of the strange infantile type of Taras with which we are dealing, in which case it singularly recalls the mystic cup stretched forth by the infant Iacchos on the votive Tarentine terra-cottas. A still more unfailing accompaniment, however, of this impersonation of Taras is the distaff wound round with wool, which, again, suggests an interesting comparison with a figure of the infant Dionysos of the Mysteries as it occurs on an Apulian krater. On this vase, which, if not actually of Tarentine work, at least belongs to the Tarentine school of ceramic art, the mystic offspring of Kora is seen depicted as a plump child, and holding in his right hand what is described as a thyrsos, but which, with its spirally-twisted top, is hardly to be distinguished from the distaff on the coins. He is represented in a squatting attitude, half-raising himself on one knee, and with the other drawn up under him, while he props himself up on his left arm. Above him is inscribed the name Dionysos, and to the left appears the head of Persephone-Kora, accompanied by the first four letters of her mystic Samothracian name Axiokersa. Both the figure on the vase and Taras in his peculiar infantile impersonation have their hair bound up into a kind of top-knot above the forehead a feature seemingly confined to this distaff-holding type. In the case of a small Tarentine gold coin, the parallel to the figure on the vase is even closer. There the infant Taras is represented in an almost identical attitude, half raising himself on one knee and with the other bent under him, and holding the distaff in his right hand. The head on the obverse of this small gold type is probably that of Persephone.

These comparisons lead us to the conclusion that the plump infantile representation of Taras which at this time makes its first appearance in the Tarentine dies, is to be regarded as approximating to that of the mystic child Iacchos, and marks the influence of a prevalent Chthonic cult on that of the Eponymic founder. (Arthur Evans, *The horsemen of Tarentum* 89-92)

Wool was further linked with death in the Bacchic Orphic cults by Herodotos:

> The Egyptians wear linen tunics with fringes hanging about the legs, called 'calasiris' and loose white woolen mantles over these. But nothing of wool is brought into the temples, or buried with them; that is forbidden. In this they follow the same rules as the ritual called Orphic and Bacchic, but which is in truth Egyptian and Pythagorean; for neither may those initiated into these rites be

buried in woolen wrappings. There is a sacred legend about this. (*The Histories* 2.81)

A prohibition which is paralleled in Apuleius:

> Those of you here present who have been initiated into the mysteries of Father Liber know what you keep hidden at home, safe from all profane touch and the object of your silent veneration. [...] Could anyone who has any idea of religion still find it strange that a man initiated in so many divine mysteries should keep at home some tokens of recognition of the cults and should wrap them in linen cloth, the purest veil for sacred objects? For wool, the excrescence of an inert body extracted from a sheep, is already a profane garment in the prescriptions of Orpheus and Pythagoras. (*Apologia* 55-56)

Cornelius Fronto notes the high regard that linen was held in by the Romans:

> In the city there was no corner without a shrine, a holy place, a temple. Besides, many books of linen were to be found in the temples, and the linen was of religious significance. (*Ad Marcum Caesarem* 4.4)

Noting some of the other uses of linen by the Romans, Eli Edward Burriss writes:

> It is possible that the linen on the breastplate of a Roman soldier had magical significance, probably warding off the spirits of the enemies slain in battle. The rolls containing the names of the magistrates, which were kept in the temple of Juno Moneta, were called "linen books." Again, a Roman consul who had won a victory over the Samnites forced the vanquished enemy to serve in his army, using novel religious rites at their induction. These soldiers made up his "linen legion," so called because the sacrifice of induction was made in an enclosure covered with linen; and the forms used in the ritual were read by an old priest from a linen book. The explanation of these rites is similar to that of the presence of linen on the breastplate of the Roman soldier. The soldiers were foreigners, and hence were taboo to a Roman. The rites were magical, intended to drive away evil forces which were felt to be attached to foreigners. The heralds who were entrusted with the responsibility of declaring war and making treaties were not allowed to wear linen garments. And if the wife of the Priest of

Jupiter sewed her woolen garment with a linen thread, she had to perform an atoning sacrifice. (*Taboo, Magic, Spirits: A study of primitive elements in Roman Religion* chapter III)

And the association between linen and holiness (for this is what Ariadne's name means) was noted by none other than Homer in his description of the Shield of Achilles in book 28 of the *Iliad*:

> Furthermore he wrought a green, like that which Daidalos once made in Knossos for lovely Ariadne. Hereon there danced youths and maidens whom all would woo, with their hands on one another's wrists. The maidens wore robes of light linen, and the youths well-woven shirts that were slightly oiled. The girls were crowned with garlands, while the young men had daggers of gold that hung by silver baldrics; sometimes they would dance deftly in a ring with merry twinkling feet, as it were a potter sitting at his work and making trial of his wheel to see whether it will run, and sometimes they would go all in line with one another, and much people was gathered joyously about the green. There was a bard also to sing to them and play his lyre, while two tumblers went about performing in the midst of them when the man struck up with his tune.

This fabulous greenway reminds one of the fields of the blessed Aristophanes had his chorus praise in *The Frogs*:

> Iakchos, much-loved resident of these quarters,
> – Iakchos, O Iakchos! –
> come to this field for the dance
> with your holy followers,
> setting in motion the crown
> which sits on your head, thick
> with myrtle-berries, boldly stamping the beat
> with your foot in the unrestrained
> fun-loving celebration –
> the dance overflowing with grace,
> dance sacred to the holy initiates!
>
> Wake the fiery torches which you brandish in your hands,
> – Iakchos, O Iakchos! –
> brilliant star of the all-night celebration!
> The meadow is aflame with light;
> old men's knees cavort!
> They shake off the pain

> of long years in old age
> in their holy excitement.
> Hold your light aloft
> and lead the youthful chorus, Lord,
> to the lush flowers of the sacred ground!

The labor of Proserpine which the spider sought to complete is the weaving of a new spiritual body for the deceased, as an Etruscan mirror reveals:

> Another specimen, of a Praenestine pear-shaped type but with Etruscan inscription, has the theme of the fate of Esia, a name unknown in Greco-Roman myth. E. H. Richardson argued that she was the equivalent of Ariadne, in a story of the latter's death as caused by Artemis, and many have accepted her suggestion. She is held wrapped up like a dead soul by Artumes, who displays the arrows with which the goddess is accustomed to end the lives of young girls. Next to her stand Fufluns, the Etruscan Dionysos, a bearded male with a drinking cup, and a winged Menrva. Below, coming up from the ground, appears an oracular head. We do not know its message, but most likely it relates to the fate of Esia. It may be that Fufluns will receive her and bestow immortality upon her. Whatever the message, Fufluns and Menrva seem to react strongly: Menrva throws up both hands in a gesture of surprise (or dismay?) and Fufluns also raises one hand. We shall observe these gestures again in other scenes of individuals who are receiving a prophecy. (Nancy de Grummond in *Mirrors, Marriage and Mystery*)

Which is very wet work indeed:

> Let the stony bowls, then, and the amphorae be symbols of the aquatic nymphs. For these are, indeed, the symbols of Dionysos, but their composition is fictile, i.e., consists of baked earth, and these are friendly to the vine, the gift of god; since the fruit of the vine is brought to a proper maturity by the celestial fire of the sun. But the stony bowls and amphorae are in the most eminent degree adapted to the nymphs who preside over the water that flows from rocks. And to souls that descend into generation and are occupied in corporeal energies, what symbol can be more appropriate than those instruments pertaining to weaving? Hence, also, the poet ventures to say, "that on these, the nymphs weave purple webs, admirable to the view." For the formation of the flesh is on and about the bones, which in the bodies of animals resemble stones. Hence these instruments of weaving consist of stone, and not of any other

matter. But the purple webs will evidently be the flesh which is woven from the blood. For purple woollen garments are tinged from blood and wool is dyed from animal juice. The generation of flesh, also, is through and from blood. Add, too, that the body is a garment with which the soul is invested, a thing wonderful to the sight, whether this refers to the composition of the soul, or contributes to the colligation of the soul (to the whole of a visible essence). Thus, also, Persephone, who is the inspective guardian of everything produced from seed, is represented by Orpheus as weaving a web and the heavens are called by the ancients a veil, in consequence of being, as it were, the vestment of the celestial gods. (Porphyry, *On the Cave of the Nymphs* 6)

Work she was well suited to, for her father was a *phoinekes* as Ovid relates:

> The girl was not known for her place of birth, or family, but for her skill. Her father, Idmon of Colophon, dyed the absorbent wool purple, with Phocaean *murex*. Her mother was dead. She too had been of humble birth, and the father the same. Nevertheless, though she lived in a modest home, in little Hypaepa, Arachne had gained a name for artistry throughout the cities of Lydia. Often the nymphs of Mount Tmolus deserted their vine-covered slopes, and the nymphs of the River Pactolus deserted their waves, to examine her wonderful workmanship. It was not only a joy to see the finished cloths, but also to watch them made: so much beauty added to art.

Mela the Golden Apples

The penultimate Toy (mentioned in the Orphic poet, Clement and Arnobius) is in Greek Μῆλα and Latin *mālum*, the apple. This is – after the grape, fig and pomegranate – perhaps *the* fruit most commonly associated with Dionysos:

> That Dionysos is also the discoverer of the apple is attested by Theokritos of Syracuse, in words something like these: 'Storing the apples of Dionysos in the folds at my bosom, and wearing on my head white poplar, sacred bough of Herakles.' And Neoptolemos the Parian, in the *Dionysiad*, records on his own authority that apples as well as all other fruits were discovered by Dionysos. (*Athenaios, Deipnosophistai 3.82d*)

For Jane Ellen Harrison, Dionysos was more than just the god of the vine, he was "Dendrites, Tree-god, and a plant god in a far wider sense. He is god of the fig-tree, Sykites; he is Kissos, god of the ivy; he is Anthios, god of all blossoming things; he is Phytalmios, god of growth" (*Prolegomena* page 426).

In short, he is the god of the impulse of life in nature, a god of growth and the green earth:

> Now as to the rites of Liber, whom they have set over liquid seeds, and therefore not only over the liquors of fruits, among which wine holds, so to speak, the primacy, but also over the seeds of animals:— as to these rites, I am unwilling to undertake to show to what excess of turpitude they had reached, because that would entail a

lengthened discourse, though I am not unwilling to do so as a demonstration of the proud stupidity of those who practice them. Varro says that certain rites of Liber were celebrated in Italy which were of such unrestrained wickedness that the shameful parts of the male were worshipped at crossroads in his honour. Nor was this abomination transacted in secret that some regard at least might be paid to modesty, but was openly and wantonly displayed. For during the festival of Liber this obscene member, placed on a little trolley, was first exhibited with great honour at the crossroads in the countryside, and then conveyed into the city itself. But in the town of Lavinium a whole month was devoted to Liber alone, during the days of which all the people gave themselves up to the must dissolute conversation, until that member had been carried through the forum and brought to rest in its own place; on which unseemly member it was necessary that the most honorable matron should place a wreath in the presence of all the people. Thus, forsooth, was the god Liber to be appeased in order for the growth of seeds. Thus was enchantment (*fascinatio*) to be driven away from fields, even by a matron's being compelled to do in public what not even a harlot ought to be permitted to do in a theatre, if there were matrons among the spectators. (Augustine, *De Civitate Dei* 7.21)

Whenever Dionysos appears, he does so attended by wild vegetation, whether it is with the vines of ivy and lush grapes he wears in his hair (*Orphic Hymn* 30), or that entwines itself around pillars and altars (Euripides' *Antiope* 203), a face appearing in a plane tree that has been split asunder (Kern's *Inschr. von M.* 215), or in a burst of beautiful flowers (Pindar fr.75). When Dionysos finally reveals himself in fullness to the Tyrrhenian pirates, it is through vegetation:

> Then in an instant a vine, running along the topmost edge of the sail, sprang up and sent out its branches in every direction heavy with thick-hanging clusters of grapes, and around the mast cloud dark-leaved ivy, rich in blossoms and bright with ripe berries, and garlands crowned every tholepin. (*Homeric Hymn* 7)

Carl Kerényi believed that intoxication was not the essential core of the religion of Dionysos, but rather the "quiet, powerful, vegetative element which ultimately engulfed even the ancient theaters, as at Cumae" (*Dionysos*, page xxiv) – as if there was a difference between the two.

It was through the apple that Dionysos entered the American mythic consciousness by way of the guise of John Chapman, a disciple of Emanuel Swedenborg who held strongly mystical and pantheistic beliefs and felt an abhorrence for modern civilization. Better known to history as Johnny

Appleseed, culture-bringer and savior of the pioneers, in truth he shunned the company of his fellow humans, preferring animals and trees like all proper Orphics; as soon as settlements encroached upon his territory he'd pick up and move on to the next site, leaving his orchards behind for the hungry settlers. Of course, what those settlers were hungry for wasn't fruit but alcohol, since the apples Johnny planted were so small and bitter that their only use was in brewing strong cider or applejack, a necessary substitute in a land where the vine initially did not thrive:

> Teaching men how to ferment the juice of the grape, Dionysus had brought civilization the gift of wine. This was more or less the same gift Johnny Appleseed was bringing to the frontier: because American grapes weren't sweet enough to be fermented successfully, the apple served as the American grape, cider the American wine. But as I delved deeper into the myth of Dionysus, I realized there was much more to his story, and the strangely changeable god who began to come into focus bore a remarkable resemblance to John Chapman. Or at least to Johnny Appleseed, who, I became convinced, is Dionysus's American son. Like Johnny Appleseed, Dionysus was a figure of the fluid margins, slipping back and forth between the realms of wildness and civilization, man and woman, man and god, beast and man ... The flight from civilization back to nature in America tends to be a solitary and ascetic pursuit, having more to do with wilderness than wildness. Johnny Appleseed was very much an *American* Dionysus – innocent and mild. In this he may have helped establish the benign, see-no-evil mood that characterizes the Dionysian strain in American culture, from transcendentalist Concord to the Summer of Love. (Michael Pollan, *The Botany of Desire*)

In Johnny's old New England stomping grounds, a young H. P. Lovecraft had his first brush with the supernatural:

> When about seven or eight I was a genuine pagan, so intoxicated with the beauty of Greece that I acquired a belief in the old gods and nature sprits. I have in literal truth built altars to Pan, Apollo, and Athena, and have watched for dryads and satyrs in the woods and fields at dusk. Once I firmly thought I beheld some kind of sylvan creatures dancing under autumnal oaks; a kind of 'religious experience' as true in its way as the subjective ecstasies of a Christian. If a Christian tell me he has felt the reality of his Jesus or Jahveh, I can reply that I have seen hoofed Pan and the sisters of the Hesperian Phaëthusa. (*Confession of Unfaith*)

Dionysos' apples, after all, aren't just any apples, as W. K. C. Guthrie reminds us:

> Nothing, we admit, is more likely to attract a child than the present of golden apples, yet it seems a little extravagant to send to the farthest confines of the world for a mythical treasure when the same purpose, it seems, could be accomplished with dolls and knucklebones. Perhaps then we may allow ourselves to remember that the apples of the Hesperides were symbols of immortality, and that Dionysos was to be born again after his murder, and by his death was to ensure the hope of immortality for the race of human beings which was to follow him. (*Orpheus and Greek Religion* pg 123)

Servius preserves the tradition, first found in Hesiod, that the Hesperides were children of Night:

> Hesiod says that these Hesperides, daughters of Nyx, guarded the golden apples beyond Okeanos, 'Aigle and Erytheia and ox-eyed Hesperethoosa.' (*Commentary on Vergil's Aeneid 4. 484*)

While Diodoros Sikeliotes preserves a contrary tradition, first found in Pherekydes of Syros, that made them daughters of the Titan Atlas:

> Now Hesperos begat a daughter named Hesperis, who he gave in marriage to his brother Atlas and after whom the land was given the name Hesperitis; and Atlas begat by her seven daughters, who were named after their father Atlantides, and after their mother Hesperides. (*Library of History 4.26.2*)

According to Pherekydes there was something so dangerously alluring about these golden apples that even the Hesperides who had been charged with their protection could not resist plucking them:

> The constellation Serpens is Ladon, said to have guarded the golden apples of the Hesperides, and after Hercules killed him, to have been put by Juno among the stars, because at her instigation Hercules set out for him. He is considered the usual watchman of the gardens of Juno. Pherecydes says that when Jupiter wed Juno, Terra came, bearing branches with golden apples, and Juno, in admiration, asked Terra to plant them in her gardens near distant Mount Atlas. When Atlas' daughters kept picking the apples from the trees, Juno is said to have placed this guardian there. (*Hyginus, Astronomica 2. 3*)

Which makes their involvement in the conception of Dionysos' mother rather interesting:

> There, as they say, by the Tritonian Lake, Kadmos the wanderer lay with rosycheek Harmonia, and the Nymphai Hesperides made a song for them, and Kypris together with the Erotes decked out a fine bed for the wedding, hanging in the bridal chamber golden fruit from the Nymphai's garden, a worthy lovegift for the bride; rich clusters of their leaves Harmonia and Kadmos twined through their hair, amid the abundance of their bridechamber, in place of the wedding-roses. Still more dainty the bride appeared wearing these golden gifts, the boon of golden Aphrodite. Her mother's father the stooping Libyan Atlas awoke a tune of the heavenly harp to join the revels, and with tripping foot he twirled the heavens round like a ball, while he sang a stave of harmony himself not far away. (*Nonnos, Dionysiaka 13.333 ff*)

For one of Semele's defining characteristics was her exceptional beauty, as Diodoros relates:

> Semele was loved by Zeus because of her beauty, but since he had his intercourse with her secretly and without speech she thought that the god despised her; consequently she made the request of him that he come to her embraces in the same manner as in his approaches to Hera. Accordingly, Zeus visited her in a way befitting a god, accompanied by thundering and lightning, revealing himself to her as he embraced her; but Semele, who was pregnant and unable to endure the majesty of the divine presence, brought forth the babe untimely and was herself slain by the fire. Thereupon Zeus, taking up the child, handed it over to the care of Hermes, and ordered him to take it to the cave in Nysa where he should deliver it to the Nymphai. (*4.2.1*)

A beauty that was not only responsible for her own destruction, but that of her nephew as well:

> Aktaion was later eaten up on Kithairon by his own dogs. According to Akousilaos he met his end in this manner because he enraged Zeus by courting the fair Semele. (*Apollodoros, Bibliotheka 3.31*)

Which naturally calls to mind the devastation wrought by Eris:

> Eris was enraged at being turned away from the wedding of Peleus and Thetis, and now she bethought her of the golden apples of the Hesperides. Thence Eris took the fruit that would become a harbinger of war, even the apple, and devised a scheme of signal

> woes. Whirling her arm she hurled into the banquet the primal seed of turmoil and disturbed the choir of goddesses. Hera, glorying to be the spouse and to share the bed of Zeus, rose up amazed, and would fain have seized it. And Kypris, as being more excellent than all, desired to have the apple, for that it is the treasure of the Erotes. But Hera would not give it up and Athena would not yield.
> (*Colluthus, Rape of Helen 58 ff*)

And also the serpent in the garden who offered Eve the tempting apple, as Clement exhorted the Greeks:

> The Bakchai hold their orgies in honour of the mad Dionysos, celebrating their sacred frenzy by the eating of raw flesh, and go through the distribution of the parts of butchered victims crowned with snakes, shrieking out the name of that Eva by whom error came into the world. The symbol of the Bacchic orgies is a consecrated serpent. Moreover, according to the strict interpretation of the Hebrew term, the name Hevia, aspirated, signifies a female serpent.

The forbidden fruit of the serpent probably wasn't our apple, unknown in Palestine at the time of the Bible's composition, but it became so in the popular imagination because of a play on the Latin words *mālum* (an apple) and *mălum* (an evil): the Latin of Genesis 2:17 "But of the tree of the knowledge of good and evil you shall not eat," is *De ligno autem scientiæ* **bonum et malum** *ne comedas*.

Olympiodoros, one of the last philosophers of antiquity, gives the final quest of Herakles an almost Judeo-Christian interpretation in his *Commentary on Plato's Gorgias*:

> And on this account Herakles is said to have accomplished his last labor in the Hesperian regions; signifying by this, that having vanquished a dark and earthly life he afterward lived in day, that is, in truth and light.

It's interesting to compare this and the relationship Jews and Christians have to their wisdom-bringing serpent with his counterpart in earlier Greek, and especially Bacchic Orphic, myth:

> The Argonauts found the sacred plot where, till the day before, the serpent Ladon, a son of the Libyan soil, had kept watch over the golden apples in the Garden of Atlas, while close at hand and busy at their tasks the Hesperides sang their lovely song. But now the snake, struck down by Herakles, lay by the trunk of the apple-tree.

Only the tip of his tail was still twitching; from the head down, his dark spine showed not a sign of life. His blood had been poisoned by arrows steeped in the gall of the Hydra Lernaia, and flies perished in the festering wounds.

Close by, with their white arms flung over their golden heads, the Hesperides were wailing as the Argonauts approached. The whole company came on them suddenly, and in a trice the Nymphai turned to dust and earth on the spot where they had stood. Orpheus, seeing the hand of Heaven in this, addressed a prayer to them on behalf of his comrades : 'Beautiful and beatific Powers, Queens indeed, be kind to us, whether Olympos or the underworld counts you among its goddesses, or whether you prefer the name of Solitary Nymphai. Come, blessed Spirits, Daughters of Okeanos, make yourselves manifest to our expectant eyes and lead us to a place where we can quench this burning, never-ending thirst with fresh water springing from a rock or gushing from the ground. And if ever we bring home our ship into an Achaian port, we will treat you as we treat the greatest goddesses, showing our gratitude with innumerable gifts of wine and offerings at the festal board.'

Orpheus sobbed as he prayed. But the Nymphai were still at hand, and they took pity on the suffering men. They wrought a miracle. First, grass sprung up from the ground, then long shoots appeared above the grass, and in a moment three saplings, tall, straight and in full leaf, were growing there. Hespere became a poplar; Erytheis an elm; Aigle a sacred willow. Yet they were still themselves; the trees could not conceal their former shapes--that was the greatest wonder of all. And now the Argonauts heard Aigle in her gentle voice tell them what they wished to know.

'You have indeed been fortunate,' she said. 'There was a man here yesterday, an evil man, who killed the watching Snake, stole our golden apples, and is gone. To us he brought unspeakable sorrow; to you release from suffering. He was a savage brute, hideous to look at; a cruel man, with glaring eyes and scowling face. He wore the skin of an enormous lion and carried a great club of olive-wood and the bow and arrows with which he shot our monster here. It appeared that he, like you, had come on foot and was parched with thirst. For he rushed about the place in search of water; but with no success, till he found the rock that you see over there near to the Tritonian lagoon. Then it occurred to him, or he was prompted by a god, to tap the base of the rock. He struck it with his foot, water gushed out, and he fell on his hands and chest and drank greedily from the cleft till, with his head down like a beast in the fields, he had filled his mighty paunch.'

> The Minyai were delighted. They ran off in happy haste towards the place where Aigle had pointed out the spring. (Apollonios Rhodios, *Argonautika* 4.1390ff)

Part of what I love about Apollonios' treatment of this myth is that it places the focus peripheral to what would conventionally be considered the action, as his contemporary Kallimachos also does in the *Hekale*. The great heroic deed is done and Herakles lumbers off to commence a life of adventure and that'd be it as far as most people are concerned. But that wasn't it for the Hesperides: no, it's just the start of the story of their life without Ladon, who had been both their protector and companion. How differently they must have seen this "monster," daily interacting with and depending on him. To them it is Herakles who is the villain! For with Ladon's death their land has been deprived of its source of supernatural vitality. When the Argonauts first meet the Nymphs of the West, land of the Sun's Descent, they were in the process of dissolving into dust and barren earth and it was only Orpheus' song that brought them back to some semblance of their selves.

In fact, in another myth it's said that Herakles even returned to pay restitution for the slaying of the serpent by gifting the Hesperides the horn of a bull-god:

> When Achelous fought with Hercules to win Dejanira in marriage, he changed himself into a bull. Hercules tore off his horn, presenting it to the Hesperides or the Nymphae, and the goddesses filled it with fruits and called it Horn of Plenty (*cornucopia*). (*Hyginus, Fabulae 31*)

This Deïaneira, by the way, was the fruit of an adulterous affair:

> When Liber had come as a guest to Oeneus, son of Parthaon, he fell in love with the man's wife Althaea, daughter of Thestius. When Oeneus realized this, he voluntarily left the city and pretended to be performing sacred rites. But Liber lay with Althaea, who became mother of Dejanira. To Oeneus, because of his generous hospitality, he gave the vine as a gift, and showed him how to plant it, and decreed that its fruit should be called '*oinos*' from the name of his host. (Hyginus, *Fabulae* 129)

Dionysos is the embodiment of the life-force – ζωή as Carl Kerényi termed it – which knows only its own self-perpetuation and nothing of morality. Dionysos is the always dying, always regenerating god, as a Tarentine poet so eloquently put it:

> If any one asks who narrates this, then we shall quote the well-known senarian verse of a Tarentine poet which the ancients used to sing,"*Taurus draconem genuit, et taurum draco.*" ["The bull begot the dragon, and the dragon a bull."] (Arnobius of Sicca, *Adversus Nationes* 5.20)

A person's father may be a complete mystery, but we *always* know our mothers. And yet with Dionysos the reverse is true – Kore-Persephone (Diodoros 5.75.4) Semele (Hesiod, *Theogony* 940) Demeter (Diodoros 3.62), Dione (Scholiast on *Pind. Pyth.* 3.177), Amaltheia (Diodoros 3.67), Isis (Alexarchos, FGrH 3.324), Indus (Philostratos, *Life of Apollonios* 2.9) Lethe (Plutarch, *Symposiacs* 7.5) and Zeus among numerous others have carried the god in their wombs – like the seed at the core of an apple:

> But the Hesperian golden-apples signify the pure and incorruptible nature of that intellect or Dionysus, which is possessed by the world; for a golden-apple, according to Sallust, is a symbol of the world; and this doubtless, both on account of its external figure, and the incorruptible intellect which it contains, and with the illuminations of which it is externally adorned; since gold, on account of never being subject to rust, aptly denotes an incorruptible and immaterial nature. (Thomas Taylor, *A Dissertation on the Eleusinian and Bacchic Mysteries* page 209)

To be possessed by the world, such a grand and horrifying concept:

> If we add to this horror the ecstatic rapture, which rises up out of the same collapse of the *principium individuationis* from the innermost depths of human beings, yes, from the innermost depths of nature, then we have a glimpse into the essence of the Dionysian, which is presented to us most closely through the analogy to intoxication. Either through the influence of narcotic drink, of which all primitive men and peoples speak, or through the powerful coming on of spring, which drives joyfully through all of nature, that Dionysian excitement arises. As its power increases, the subjective fades into complete forgetfulness of self. In the German Middle Ages under the same power of Dionysus constantly growing hordes waltzed from place to place, singing and dancing. In that St. John's and St. Vitus's dancing we recognize the Bacchic chorus of the Greeks once again, and its precursors in Asia Minor, right back to Babylon and the orgiastic Sacaea. (Friedrich Nietzsche, *The Birth of Tragedy*)

We get a glimpse of this collapse in Carl Gustav Jung's study of the paintings of Pablo Picasso:

And just as Faust is embroiled in murderous happenings and reappears in changed form, so Picasso changes shape and reappears in the underworld form of the tragic Harlequin – a motif that runs through numerous paintings. It may be remarked in passing that Harlequin is an ancient chthonic god. The descent into ancient times has been associated ever since Homer's day with the Nekyia. Faust turns back to the crazy primitive world of the witches' sabbath and to a chimerical vision of classical antiquity. Picasso conjures up crude, earthy shapes, grotesque and primitive, and resurrects the soullessness of ancient Pompeii in a cold, glittering light – even Giulio Romano could not have done worse! Seldom or never have I had a patient who did not go back to neolithic art forms or revel in evocations of Dionysian orgies. Harlequin wanders like Faust through all these forms, though sometimes nothing betrays his presence but his wine, his lute, or the bright lozenges of his jester's costume. And what does he learn on his wild journey through man's millennial history? What quintessence will he distil from this accumulation of rubbish and decay, from these half-born or aborted possibilities of form and colour? What symbol will appear as the final cause and meaning of all this. In view of the dazzling versatility of Picasso, one hardly dares to hazard a guess, so for the present I would rather speak of what I have found in my patients' material. The Nekyia is no aimless and purely destructive fall into the abyss, but a meaningful *katabasis eis antron*, a descent into the cave of initiation and secret knowledge. The journey through the psychic history of mankind has as its object the restoration of the whole man, by awakening the memories in the blood. The descent to the Mothers enabled Faust to raise up the sinfully whole human being – Paris united with Helen – that *homo totus* who was forgotten when contemporary man lost himself in one-sidedness. It is he who at all times of upheaval has caused the tremor of the upper world, and always will. This man stands opposed to the man of the present, because he is the one who ever is as he was, whereas the other is what he is only for the moment. With my patients, accordingly, the *katabasis* and *katalysis* are followed by a recognition of the bipolarity of human nature and of the necessity of conflicting pairs of opposites. After the symbols of madness experienced during the period of disintegration there follow images which represent the coming together of the opposites: light/dark, above/below, white/black, male/female, etc. In Picasso's latest paintings, the motif of the union of opposites is seen very clearly in their direct juxtaposition. One painting (although traversed by numerous lines of fracture) even contains the conjunction of the light and dark anima. The strident, uncompromising, even brutal colours of the latest period reflect the tendency of the unconscious to master the conflict by violence (colour = feeling). This state of things in the psychic development of a patient is neither the end nor the goal. It represents only a broadening of his outlook, which now embraces the whole of man's moral, bestial, and spiritual nature without as yet shaping it into a living unity. Picasso's drame interieur has developed up to this last point before the denouement. As to the future Picasso, I would rather not try my hand at prophecy, for this inner adventure is a hazardous affair and can lead at any moment to a standstill or to a catastrophic bursting asunder of the conjoined opposites. Harlequin is a tragically ambiguous figure, even though – as the initiated may discern – he already bears on his costume the symbols of the next stage of development. He is indeed the hero who must pass through the perils of Hades, but will he succeed? That is a question I cannot answer. Harlequin gives me the creeps – he is too reminiscent of that 'motley fellow, like a buffoon' in Zarathustra, who jumped over the unsuspecting rope-dancer (another Pagliacci) and thereby brought about his death. Zarathustra then spoke the words that were to prove so horrifyingly true of Nietzsche himself: 'Your soul will be dead even sooner than your body: fear nothing more than I.' Who the buffoon is, is made plain as he cries out to the rope-dancer, his weaker alter ego: 'To one better than yourself you bar the way.' He is the greater personality who bursts the shell, and this shell is sometimes – the brain. (*Neue Zürcher Zeitung* 1932)

But even more clearly in the Dionysian dreams of his patients:

I saw a beautiful youth with golden cymbals, dancing and leaping in joy and abandonment... Finally he fell to the ground and buried his face in the flowers. Then he sank into the lap of a very old mother. After a time he got up and jumped into the water, where he sported like a dolphin... I saw that his hair was golden. Now we were leaping together, hand in hand. So we came to a gorge... In leaping the gorge the youth falls into the chasm. X is left alone and comes to a river where a white sea-horse is waiting for her with a golden boat. X found the youth in the lap of the mother so impressive that she painted a picture of it. The figure is the same as in item i; only, instead of the grain of wheat in her hand, there is the body of the youth lying completely exhausted in the lap of the gigantic mother. There now follows a sacrifice of sheep, during which a game of ball is likewise played with the sacrificial animal. The participants smear themselves with the sacrificial blood, and afterwards bathe in the pulsing gore. X is thereupon transformed into a plant. After that X comes to a den of snakes, and the snakes wind all round her. In a den of snakes beneath the sea there is a divine woman, asleep. She is shown in the picture as much larger than the others. She is wearing a blood-red garment that covers only the lower half of her body. She has dark skin, full red lips, and seems to be of great physical strength. She kisses X, who is obviously in the role of the young girl, and hands her as a present to the many men who are standing by, etc. As X emerged from the depths and saw the light again, she experienced a kind of illumination: white flames played about her head as she walked through waving fields of grain. (*The Archetypes and the Collective Unconscious* p. 188-189)

It is death that makes possible the great abundance of life, as D. H. Lawrence reflects on in *Medlars and Sorb-Apples*:

> I love you, rotten,
> Delicious rottenness.
>
> I love to suck you out from your skins
> So brown and soft and coming suave,
> So morbid, as the Italians say.
>
> What a rare, powerful, reminiscent flavour
> Comes out of your falling through the stages of decay:
> Stream within stream.
>
> Something of the same flavour as Syracusan muscat wine
> Or vulgar Marsala.
>
> Though even the word Marsala will smack of preciosity
> Soon in the pussy-foot West.
>
> What is it?
> What is it, in the grape turning raisin,
> In the medlar, in the sorb-apple.
> Wineskins of brown morbidity,
> Autumnal excrementa;
> What is it that reminds us of white gods?
>
> Gods nude as blanched nut-kernels.
> Strangely, half-sinisterly flesh-fragrant
> As if with sweat,
> And drenched with mystery.

Sorb-apples, medlars with dead crowns.

I say, wonderful are the hellish experiences
Orphic, delicate
Dionysos of the Underworld.

A kiss, and a vivid spasm of farewell, a moment's orgasm of rupture.
Then along the damp road alone, till the next turning.
And there, a new partner, a new parting, a new unfusing into twain,
A new gasp of further isolation,
A new intoxication of loneliness, among decaying, frost-cold leaves.

Going down the strange lanes of hell, more and more intensely alone,
The fibres of the heart parting one after the other
And yet the soul continuing, naked-footed, ever more vividly embodied
Like a flame blown whiter and whiter
In a deeper and deeper darkness
Ever more exquisite, distilled in separation.

So, in the strange retorts of medlars and sorb-apples
The distilled essence of hell.
The exquisite odour of leave-taking.
   Jamque vale!
Orpheus, and the winding, leaf-clogged, silent lanes of hell.

Each soul departing with its own isolation,
Strangest of all strange companions,
And best.

Medlars, sorb-apples
More than sweet
Flux of autumn
Sucked out of your empty bladders
And sipped down, perhaps, with a sip of Marsala
So that the rambling, sky-dropped grape can add its music to yours,
Orphic farewell, and farewell, and farewell
And the *ego sum* of Dionysos
The *sono io* of perfect drunkenness
Intoxication of final loneliness.

Esoptron the Mirror

As potent as the allure of the other Toys are, it is Ἔσοπτρον, the Mirror, who holds the young god fast so that his tormentors may catch and slaughter him:

> By this marriage with the heavenly dragon, the womb of Persephone swelled with living fruit and she bore Zagreus the horned babe, who by himself climbed upon the heavenly throne of Zeus and brandished lightning in his little hand. But he did not hold the throne of Zeus for long. Goaded by the fierce resentment of implacable Hera, the Titans cunningly smeared their round faces with disguising chalk (*titanos*), and while he contemplated his changeling countenance reflected in a mirror they destroyed him with an infernal knife. There where his limbs had been cut piecemeal by the Titan steel, the end of his life was the beginning of a new life as Dionysos. (Nonnos, *Dionysiaka* 6.155 ff)

For many authors, especially those of the Neoplatonic school, the entire titanic ordeal can be represented in abbreviated form by allusion to the encounter with Esoptron:

> It is said that Hephaistos made a mirror for Dionysos and that the god, seeing himself in it and contemplating his own image, decided to create all plurality. (Proklos, *Commentary on Plato's Timaios* 33b)

> Dionysos, when he saw his image reflected in the mirror, began to pursue it and so was torn to pieces. But Apollon put Dionysos back

together and brought him back to life because he was a purifying god and the true savior. (Olympiodoros, *Commentary on Plato's Phaedo* 67c)

And the mysteries in honor of Dionysos were conducted in secret; they would carry along phalli, as being the generative organs, and a mirror, as representing the translucently radiant heavens. (Ioannes Laurentios Lydos, *de Mensibus* 51)

But the souls of men see their images as if in the mirror of Dionysos and come to be on that level with a leap from above, but these too are not cut off from their own principle, and from intellect. (Plotinos, *Enneads* 4.3.12)

However, each of them gives it a slightly different meaning. In Proklos, Dionysos is prompted by contemplating his reflection to demiurgically form a world of plurality, while in Olympiodoros this creation is not an act of willed intellect, but rather a calamitous accident which causes the one to become many, a state that must be rectified by Apollon, whose name alone is a restorative (*a* not *polu* many) – a concept that hearkens back to the pantheistic vision of Plutarch in *On the E at Delphi* 9:

> As for his passage and distribution into waves and water, and earth, and stars, and nascent plants and animals, they hint at the actual change undergone as a rending and dismemberment, but name the god himself Dionysos or Zagreus or Nyktelios or Isodaites. Deaths too and vanishings do they construct, passages out of life and new births, all riddles and tales to match the changes mentioned. So they sing to Dionysos dithyrambic strains, charged with sufferings and a change wherein are wanderings and dismemberment. For Aischylos says:
>
>> In mingled cries the dithyramb should ring,
>> With Dionysos revelling, its King.

In constrast Apollon has the Paean, a set and sober music. Apollon is ever ageless and young; Dionysos has many forms and many shapes as represented in paintings and sculpture, which attribute to Apollon smoothness and order and a gravity with no admixture, but to Dionysos a blend of sport and sauciness with seriousness and frenzy:

> God that sett'st maiden's blood
> Dancing in frenzied mood,
> Blooming with pageantry!

> Evoe! we cry

So do they summon him, rightly catching his changeable character.

While in Plotinos the situation is reversed and it is the souls of men who take the plunge into matter through the Mirror of Dionysos:

> Now, Plotinus' suggestion is that our not yet embodied souls "see" themselves in matter as if in a mirror. Seduced by the delightful possibilities of the phenomenal world and the part they might play in it, the souls "jump down" without deliberation. Gazing into the mirror of matter, spontaneous and innocent desire makes our souls embark on the migration to this world: as soon as our disembodied selves behold their image, they are already 'here' while still remaining 'there.' Something quite innocent arose within them and tore them asunder. According to the Neoplatonic interpretation of the Zagreus myth, human beings are, in a sense, images of Dionysos, fleeting and fragmented appearances in his mirror. Or, to put it differently: fleeting and fragmented dispersions of divine consciousness in the mirror of matter. (Christian Wildberg, *Dionysos in the Mirror of Philosophy: Heraclitus, Plato, and Plotinus*)

Pretty heady stuff, and yet the Mirror of Dionysos likely held a different meaning for those who originally coined the term. For instance, already in Alkaios there's the assertion that wine was a mirror of mankind (fr. 104 Diehl) and a fragment attributed to Aischylos similarly states that wine is a mirror of the soul (fr. 393 *TrGF* III) – in other words, the mirror's ability to accurately reflect what is there and the distinction it draws between reality and false, distorted perception is what stood out for these men. For this reason Diogenes Laertios (2.33) recounts that Sokrates recommended the constant use of the mirror in fulfilling the Delphic injunction to Know Thyself.

However, ancient mirrors were not always very clear or trustworthy. William Smith gives a comprehensive, if somewhat dated, picture of what they were like in *A Dictionary of Greek and Roman Antiquities*:

> The mirrors of the Greeks, Romans, and Etruscans consisted almost invariably of small circular disks of metal, which could be placed upright on a table or held in the hand. Mirrors of glass are mentioned by Pliny (*Nat. Hist.* 36.66) as being made at Sidon, and from a later source (Alex. Aphrod., *Probl.* 1.132) we learn that glass mirrors were coated with tin, not, as with us, with quicksilver. No remains of such mirrors exist, however, and they were evidently little used. The usual material was bronze, i. e. an alloy of copper and tin, composed, as the analysis of various Roman mirrors has

shown (Blümner, *Technologie*, iv. p. 192), of from 19 to 32 per cent. of the latter metal. In Imperial times, the best alloy for mirrors was made at Brundisium (*Nat. Hist.* 33.45; 34.48). The majority of extant mirrors are of bronze, but some made of silver have also come down to us. A better reflexion was supposed to be given when the plate of silver was thick (Vitr. 7.3). At first, the silver was very pure, but metal of inferior quality was afterwards employed (Plin. *Nat. Hist.* 33.45). Cheap imitations were manufactured, and some extant mirrors having the appearance of silver are in reality only plated with that metal, or are composed of a mixture of copper and lead (Friederichs, *Berl. ant. Bildw.* ii. p. 86). There is no mention of mirrors in Homer, and the earliest Greek mirrors extant are not earlier than circ. B.C. 500. The prototype of the Greek mirror must, on our present evidence, be looked for in Egypt. But from the time of the Attic tragedians onwards mirrors are frequently mentioned in literature (Aesch. in Stob. *Serm.* 18.13; Eur. *Tro.* 1107; *Medea*, 1161; Onet. 1112;--Xen. *Cyr.* 7.1, § 2, &c.), and they are often represented on the monuments. On the vase-paintings female attendants are seen holding them before their mistresses, and among the Greek terra-cottas are figures of women holding circular mirrors while arranging their hair (*Gazette arch.* 1878, pl. 10 = Baumeister, Denkm, art. "*Spiegel*," fig. 1775; Gaz. arch. 1880, p. 39).

We get an even better sense of the distorted reflections of ancient mirrors in Pausanias' account of the sanctuary of Despoina in Lykosoura:

> These too are works of Damophon. Demeter carries a torch in her right hand; her other hand she has laid upon Despoina. Despoina has on her knees a staff and what is called the box, which she holds in her right hand. On both sides of the throne are images. By the side of Demeter stands Artemis wrapped in the skin of a deer, and carrying a quiver on her shoulders, while in one hand she holds a torch, in the other two serpents; by her side a bitch, of a breed suitable for hunting, is lying down. By the image of Despoina stands Anytos, represented as a man in armour. Those about the sanctuary say that Despoina was brought up by Anytos, who was one of the Titans, as they are called. The first to introduce Titans into poetry was Homer, representing them as gods down in what is called Tartaros; the lines are in the passage about Hera's oath. From Homer the name of the Titans was taken by Onomakritos, who in the orgies he composed for Dionysos made the Titans the authors of the god's sufferings. The story of the Kouretes, who are represented under the images, and that of the Korybantes (a different race from the Kouretes), carved in relief upon the base, I know, but pass them

by. The Arcadians bring into the sanctuary the fruit of all cultivated trees except the pomegranate. On the right as you go out of the temple there is a mirror fitted into the wall. If anyone looks into this mirror, he will see himself very dimly indeed or not at all, but the actual images of the gods and the throne can be seen quite clearly. When you have gone up a little, beside the temple of Despoina on the right is what is called the Hall, where the Arcadians celebrate mysteries, and sacrifice to Despoina many victims in generous fashion. Every man of them sacrifices what he possesses. But he does not cut the throats of the victims, as is done in other sacrifices; each man chops off a limb of the sacrifice, just that which happens to come to hand. Despoina the Arcadians worship more than any other god, declaring that she is a daughter of Poseidon and Demeter. Despoina ("Mistress") is her surname among the many, just as they surname Demeter's daughter by Zeus Kore ("the Maid"). But whereas the real name of Kore is Persephone, as Homer and Pamphos before him say in their poems, the real name of Despoina I am afraid to write to the uninitiated. (*Description of Greece* 8.37.4-9)

And yet, well before those dusty philosophers got their hands on the myth we find a plunge into another world through a reflective surface associated with Dionysos. Most often this other world is the underworld – which could be under either land or water, as Dimitrios Paleothodoros relates in his study on *Dionysos and the Tyrrhenian Pirates*:

> The maddened sailors are conquered by the desire to dance and as soon as they come into contact with the waves, they undergo a radical transformation leading to a new existence, which may be plausibly paralleled to the loss of the self experienced by the followers of Dionysus. Both as a punishment and a salvation from madness and terror, the transformation of pirates into dolphins marks their introduction into the retinue of the god. Etruscan monuments provide a further link between Dionysus and the dolphins. It has been noted recently that the appearance of dolphins leaping into the sea on Etruscan wall-paintings and mirrors of the late archaic period does not have a decorative function, but betrays an eschatological message. Since the tomb is regarded as a place of mediation between the world of the living and the world of the dead, the idea of putting friezes of dolphins leaping into the sea in the lower part of wall-paintings and mirrors found in tombs might have served as a point of juncture between the two worlds. The act of leaping into the deep sea is regarded, in funerary iconography

and symbolism, as an act of passage from the world of the living into the world of the dead.

And as we saw earlier, a Dionysian leap can lead to a Dionysian fall, and with it a sentence of death, as Katharina Wesselmann notes in *Madness: The complexity of morals in the light of myth and cult*:

> There remains the tradition of the wounded leg connecting Herodotus' stories of Miltiades, Cambyses and Cleomenes, and the myth of mad Lycurgus fighting the god Dionysus. This element leads us even further. The metaphor of falling and jumping—Cambyses jumps on his horse when injuring his thigh (3.64.3), Miltiades jumps from the wall (6.134.2), both actions go wrong and therefore turn into falls—is often used in the context of madness, such as in Euripides' *Bacchae*, when the chorus sings of the fall of Dionysus after running with the thiasos (136–137). This fall has been interpreted as mirroring the moment where the ecstatic bacchant falls down and is possessed by the god (Dodds 1960). In this context, the song of the madness-inducing Erinyes in Aeschylus' *Eumenides* is interesting, too:
>
>> With a great leap from above
>> I bring down my foot's heavy-falling force.
>> My limbs make even fast runners fall:
>> a terrible disaster.
>> And as he falls, he knows nothing, in mad folly. (372-377)
>
> Jumping and falling are interchangeable; the foot is 'heavy-falling' in an active 'leap'. Likewise, Cambyses and Miltiades can be seen as actively jumping into a passively suffered misfortune, and therefore as a metaphor for the structure of *mania*-reversal in general: active aggression becomes passively suffered autoaggression, jumping turns into falling.

When the Etruscans wished to consecrate something like a mirror to the underworld powers it had to be ritually broken first:

> The mirror in the *corredo* of an Etruscan bride was part of the wedding ritual. At her death, it was part of another ritual, when she took it to the grave with her. It was then dedicated to *L'espace da la Mort*. Sometimes, by bending the handle or scratching across the reflecting surface the word *suthina* "for the grave" it was effectively destroyed for the living, and consecrated to a different level of reality – the world of the dead, of ancestors, and of the gods. After the public rituals of wedding and funeral, the mirror was put in a

private place – the home or the grave – where it symbolized marriage and home, children, the life of a *mater familias*. (Larissa Bonfante, *Etruscan mirrors and the grave*)

That's because things are very different on the other side, as Saint Paul aptly noted in his *First Letter to the Corinthians*:

> If I speak in the tongues of men or of angels, but do not have love, I am only a resounding gong or a clanging cymbal. If I have the gift of prophecy and can fathom all mysteries and all knowledge, and if I have a faith that can move mountains, but do not have love, I am nothing. If I give all I possess to the poor and give over my body to hardship that I may boast, but do not have love, I gain nothing. [...] Love never fails. But where there are prophecies, they will cease; where there are tongues, they will be stilled; where there is knowledge, it will pass away. For we know in part and we prophesy in part, but when completeness comes, what is in part disappears. When I was a child, I talked like a child, I thought like a child, I reasoned like a child. When I became a man, I put the ways of childhood behind me. For now we see through a glass, darkly; but then face to face: now I know in part; but then shall I know even as also I am known.

Those with a clear eye should be able to spot most of the Toys of Dionysos in this passage. That is not accidental, as Richard Seaford notes:

> Why should the image 'for now we see through a glass darkly, etc.' be thought to be analogous to the passage from childhood to adulthood? Paul alludes to the Pagan Mysteries, or at the least uses language derived from them: a Greek audience would be expected to understand. The Greek for 'through a glass darkly' is *di esoptrou en ainigmati*: we see 'through a mirror in a riddle'; a curious conjunction of images. The passages that have been adduced from the Judaic tradition are inadequate to explain this passage fully. The important point is that the function of the mirror in this context is negative, it is an agent of obscurity: now we see merely through the mirror, but then we shall see directly, face to face.

Henry Liddell in his *Greek-English Lexicon* notes that Paul here uses the verb form of *esoptron* which is a biblical hapax and attested rarely in Classical and Hellenistic literature. Close (perhaps *too close*) family friend and fellow Oxford don Charles Lutwidge Dodgson described, under the guise of Lewis Carroll, a fateful trip taken by Henry's youngest daughter in *Through the Looking-Glass*:

And here I wish I could tell you half the things Alice used to say, beginning with her favourite phrase 'Let's pretend.' She had had quite a long argument with her sister only the day before—all because Alice had begun with 'Let's pretend we're kings and queens;' and her sister, who liked being very exact, had argued that they couldn't, because there were only two of them, and Alice had been reduced at last to say, 'Well, YOU can be one of them then, and I'LL be all the rest.' And once she had really frightened her old nurse by shouting suddenly in her ear, 'Nurse! Do let's pretend that I'm a hungry hyaena, and you're a bone.' But this is taking us away from Alice's speech to the kitten. 'Let's pretend that you're the Red Queen, Kitty! Do you know, I think if you sat up and folded your arms, you'd look exactly like her. Now do try, there's a dear!' And Alice got the Red Queen off the table, and set it up before the kitten as a model for it to imitate: however, the thing didn't succeed, principally, Alice said, because the kitten wouldn't fold its arms properly. So, to punish it, she held it up to the Looking-glass, that it might see how sulky it was—'and if you're not good directly,' she added, 'I'll put you through into Looking-glass House. How would you like THAT?'

'Now, if you'll only attend, Kitty, and not talk so much, I'll tell you all my ideas about Looking-glass House. First, there's the room you can see through the glass—that's just the same as our drawing room, only the things go the other way. I can see all of it when I get upon a chair—all but the bit behind the fireplace. Oh! I do so wish I could see THAT bit! Well then, the books are something like our books, only the words go the wrong way; I know that, because I've held up one of our books to the glass, and then they hold up one in the other room. How would you like to live in Looking-glass House, Kitty? I wonder if they'd give you milk in there? Perhaps Looking-glass milk isn't good to drink—But oh, Kitty! now we come to the passage. You can just see a little PEEP of the passage in Looking-glass House, if you leave the door of our drawing-room wide open: and it's very like our passage as far as you can see, only you know it may be quite different on beyond. Oh, Kitty! how nice it would be if we could only get through into Looking-glass House! I'm sure it's got, oh! such beautiful things in it! Let's pretend there's a way of getting through into it, somehow, Kitty. Let's pretend the glass has got all soft like gauze, so that we can get through. Why, it's turning into a sort of mist now, I declare! It'll be easy enough to get through—' She was up on the chimney-piece while she said this, though she hardly knew how she had got there. And certainly the glass WAS beginning to melt away, just like a bright silvery mist.

> In another moment Alice was through the glass, and had jumped lightly down into the Looking-glass room. The very first thing she did was to look whether there was a fire in the fireplace, and she was quite pleased to find that there was a real one, blazing away as brightly as the one she had left behind. 'So I shall be as warm here as I was in the old room,' thought Alice: 'warmer, in fact, because there'll be no one here to scold me away from the fire. Oh, what fun it'll be, when they see me through the glass in here, and can't get at me!' Then she began looking about, and noticed that what could be seen from the old room was quite common and uninteresting, but that all the rest was as different as possible. For instance, the pictures on the wall next the fire seemed to be all alive, and the very clock on the chimney-piece (you know you can only see the back of it in the Looking-glass) had got the face of a little old man, and grinned at her.

There is something mad and a little menacing in Alice's innocent romping through the strange world on the other side of the mirror, which calls to mind Dionysos' ambling trek through the swamp in Aristophanes' *The Frogs*:

> This is a play for an Athens that has learned to read and thereby lost its innocence regarding myth and the enchantment of language — a city in which even the traditions of dramatic performance itself can be taken apart for the delectation of an audience of all-knowing readers. In this Athens, judging poetry is one strand in a wider net of social, political and cultural judgement: your taste in music and drama betrays who you are as a person. As Richard Hunter has recently shown, this play shows us the complex skein of social and aesthetic issues in which tragedy, as an institution, and the act of judging tragedy, were implicated. Like Odysseus in the epic which bears his name, or like Orpheus in search of Eurydice, Dionysus as the god of drama must go down to the Underworld, not to meet Tiresias and learn his future, but to meet the now-dead poets of the past. Among other things, *Frogs* is a love-letter to a poetic tradition that is reaching the end of its creative phase. Both Sophocles and Euripides died in the months preceding the performance. Early in the play (52-4), Dionysus tells Heracles that, reading Euripides' *Andromache*, he was suddenly seized by an almost erotic desire for the absent author; there is a sense in which *Frogs* is really about the ways we love, interpret and pass judgement on authorless texts as substitutes for the author's living voice. The underworld, as Aristophanes presents it, is recognisably the Hades of the mythological and religious traditions of Attica: we meet the familiar

gods and demons (Charon on his boat; the chorus of Eleusinian initiates). But it is also, with its innkeepers, lusty chambermaids and testy slaves, a place like the real world: the frog-chorus inhabits not only the river Styx, but the Lenaean marshes: an allusion to the festival at which the play was staged; Aeacus, the implacable mythological judge of dead souls, comes back as the doorman of a shabbily bourgeois Hell, and the poets fight out between themselves the cultural debates raging about poetry and education in the intellectual life of the democratic city. Should drama be *about* life, or should it idealise reality? What do poets actually *teach*? Should the language tragic poets use be grand or plain? If we get the answers right, dramatic poetry, it seems, can save the city. (Peter Agócs, *Aristophanes' Frogs: the end of an era*)

As true as this observation is, it doesn't do justice to the fractured personality that Dionysos demonstrates in *The Frogs*:

In *The Frogs*, the godly character of Dionysus is subverted to reveal a ridiculous buffoon, a figure of burlesque. Indeed, Dionysus is strongly parodied and shown as a pitiful creature in the first part of the drama. He engages in nonsensical jokes and word play with his slave Xanthias, which the latter does not understand. The god introduces himself to the audience under a grotesque name as "Dionysus, son of the wine-jar." In his decision to go down to Hades and fetch the recently deceased Euripides back to earth, Dionysus disguises himself in the lion-skin and club of Heracles. But in spite of the brave exterior, Dionysus still retains his effeminate manners which arouse comic laughter in Heracles, "The lion-skin on a robe of saffron silk! How comes my club to consort with high-heeled boots?" The god is further seized with abnormal fear when Heracles describes to him the dangers to be witnessed in the underworld, "…snakes and queer monsters, crowds and crowds." In fact to conceal his terror, Dionysus even assumes the name of "Heracles-the-brave." The moral cowardice of Dionysus is finally revealed when he swallows the insults of Charon, the ferryman, the latter rebuking him for his ignorance of certain things. Thus Dionysus, the patron god of drama, in whose sanctuary all tragedies and comedies were performed, is seen in the play as a contemptible braggart, a coward, morally inferior even to his slave Xanthias. This is the reason why Carlo Pascal in *Dioniso*, his study of religion and religious parody in Aristophanes comments that in *The Frogs*, "Aristophanes has stripped Dionysus of all his divine attributes; he has made him a vulgar and ridiculous man, a brash trickster…" Pascal emphasizes that Aristophanes attired Dionysus in Heracles'

clothes and made of the god a human being, foolish and lowly for the purpose of parodying him. E. Lapalus in *The Dionysus of the Frogs* concludes that Dionysus cannot be a god. "He is a coarse and lazy trickster, a man vulgar and sensual, all in all a being who has about him nothing of the divine."
[...]
The cardinal problem, a kind of inconsistency in the character of Dionysus, arises as he undergoes a striking change from the timorous, coarse figure of the first part to the grave role of an arbiter in the literary competition between Aeschylus and Euripides, towards the end of *The Frogs*. This two-fold, contradictory element inherent in Dionysus can be traced to the evolution of his figure through the ages. By the fifth century, Dionysus had come to be depicted with an effeminate appearance, blending masculine and feminine, the theatrical and the real, the foreign and the native. Such multifarious elements present in Dionysus also suggest, in a serious way, a lack of secure sense of self and identity. In *The Frogs*, Dionysus is not just a single individual but a representative of the entire Athenian community. From the very beginning, we have subtle references to this loss of individuality in the god. Dionysus sets out on his journey for Hades not dressed as himself but disguised as Heracles, complete with lion-skin and club. Thus the costume of Heracles is not just a ludicrous prop but poses a serious ironical suggestion. The combination of club, lion-skin, tragic-buskin and a woman's robe, piling as it does male, female and animal, symbolizes the uncertainty in Dionysus which in turn reflects the uncertainty in the hearts of the Athenians in those days of social and political crisis. The time when Aristophanes wrote *The Frogs*, politically, the worst elements were in control of the city; while many of the best citizens were disenfranchised or in exile, the demagogues misruled Athens. In fact we can draw a parallel between Dionysus' determination to retrieve Euripides from Hades because the earth was lacking in any first-grade tragedians to the demand of the Athenians for the recall of their favourite Alcibiades whom they wanted to give the reins of the state. The main task for Aristophanes was to strengthen the Athenian mind in this time of political crisis and turmoil. In the god Dionysus, the dramatist typifies the common man with all his comical faults, and loss of self confidence. (Ankita Mookherjee, *The comic portraiture of Dionysus in Aristophanes' Frogs: a device to revive the true spirit of Athens*)

That's right. Dionysos only seems to make the *katabasis* in pursuit of his beloved Euripides – in truth he's forgotten who he is and discovers that only in wandering through the marsh that leads below and confronting the horrors it holds, much like in the myth of the mad god and the swamp-donkey who joined the stars:

> In one part of its figure there are certain stars called Asses, pictured on the shell of the Crab by Liber with two stars only. For Liber, when madness was sent upon him by Juno, is said to have fled wildly through Thesprotia intending to reach the oracle of Dodonaean Jove to ask how he might recover his former sanity. When he came to a certain large swamp which he couldn't cross, it is said two asses met him. He caught one of them and in this way was carried across, not touching the water at all. So when he came to the temple of Dodonaean Jove, freed at once from his madness, he acknowledged his thanks to the asses and placed them among the constellations. Some say he gave a human voice to the ass which had carried him. This ass later had a contest with Priapus on a matter of physique, but was defeated and killed by him. Pitying him because of this, Liber numbered him among the stars, and so that it should be known that he did this as a god, not as a timid man fleeing from Juno, he placed him above the Crab which had been added to the stars by her kindness. (Hyginus, *Astronomica* 2.23)

As well as the Bacchic Orphic gold leaf from Petelia:

> You will find a spring on the left of the halls of Hades, and beside it a white cypress growing. Do not even go near this spring. And you will find another, from the Lake of Memory, flowing forth with cold water. In front of it are guards. You must say, 'I am the child of Ge and starry Ouranos; this you yourselves also know. I am dry with thirst and am perishing. Come, give me at once cold water flowing forth from the Lake of Memory.' And they themselves will give you to drink from the divine stream, and then thereafter you will reign with the other heroes.

This is why Esoptron can be so dangerous. It holds within it the potential to reveal to us who we truly are as well as to ensnare us in madness and illusion, as Ralph Comer's 1969 detective story *The Mirror of Dionysos* makes clear:

> 'So what,' said Lawson. 'Why all this rigmarole about photographers?' 'Because photography is the dominant art form of the present time. A cornucopia of images. And now, through electronics, a greater influence for good and evil than all the books ever written. The camera lens is the modern mirror of Dionysos and

those, like you, who use it, are the new high priests. Legend has it that the Titans were able to kill Zagreus by distracting his attention with his own distorted image in a mirror. Perhaps that is what is happening to the world. Perhaps there are those who want it to happen.' Lawson smiled. 'The medium or the message.'

The same ambiguity is felt in Jim Morrison's prophetic utterance from *The Lords and the New Creatures*:

> The subject says "I see first lots of things which dance — then everything becomes gradually connected."
>
> The world becomes an apparently infinite,
> yet possibly finite, card game.
> Image combinations,
> permutations,
> comprise the world game.
>
> "Players"-the child, the actor, and the gambler. The idea of chance is absent from the world of the child and primitive. The gambler also feels in service of an alien power. Chance is a survival of religion in the modern city, as is theater, more often cinema, the religion of possession.
>
> There are no longer "dancers," the possessed. The cleavage of men into actor and spectators is the central fact of our time. We are obsessed with heroes who live for us and whom we punish. If all the radios and televisions were deprived of their sources of power, all books and paintings burned tomorrow, all shows and cinemas closed, all the arts of vicarious existence...
>
> Windows work two ways, mirrors one way.
> You never walk through mirrors or swim through windows.
>
> We are content with the "given" in sensation's quest. We have been metamorphosised from a mad body dancing on hillsides to a pair of eyes staring in the dark.
>
> Cinema returns us to anima, religion of matter, which gives each thing its special divinity and sees gods in all things and beings. Cinema, heir of alchemy, last of an erotic science.
>
> Cinema is most totalitarian of the arts. All energy and sensation is sucked up into the skull, a cerebral erection, skull bloated with blood. Caligula wished a single neck for all his subjects that he

could behead a kingdom with one blow. Cinema is this transforming agent. The body exists for the sake of the eyes; it becomes a dry stalk to support these two soft insatiable jewels.

Few would defend a small view of Alchemy as "Mother of Chemistry", and confuse its true goal with those external metal arts. Alchemy is an erotic science, involved in buried aspects of reality, aimed at purifying and transforming all being and matter. Not to suggest that material operations are ever abandoned. The adept holds to both the mystical and physical work.

They can picture love affairs of chemicals and stars, a romance of stones, or the fertility of fire. Strange, fertile correspondences the alchemists sensed in unlikely orders of being. Between men and planets, plants and gestures, words and weather.

More or less, we're all afflicted with the psychology of the voyeur. Not in a strictly clinical or criminal sense, but in our whole physical and emotional stance before the world. Whenever we seek to break this spell of passivity, our actions are cruel and awkward and generally obscene, like an invalid who has forgotten to walk.

Look where we worship. We all live in the city.

The city forms- often physically, but inevitably psychically- a circle. A Game. A ring of death with sex at its center. Drive towards outskirts of city suburbs. At the edge of discover zones of sophisticated vice and boredom, child prostitution. But in the grimy ring immediately surrounding the daylight business district exists the only real crowd life of our mound, the only street life, night life. Diseased specimens in dollar hotels, low boarding houses, bars, pawn shops, burlesques and brothels, in dying arcades which never die, in streets and streets of all-night cinemas.

The Lords. Events take place beyond our knowledge or control. Our lives are lived for us. We can only try to enslave others. But gradually, special perceptions are being developed. The idea of the "Lords" is beginning to form in some minds. We should enlist them into bands of perceivers to tour the labyrinth during their mysterious nocturnal appearances. The Lords have secret entrances, and they know disguises. But they give themselves away in minor ways. Too much glint of light in the eye. A wrong gesture. Too long and curious a glance.

The Lords appease us with images. They give us books, concerts, galleries, shows, cinemas. Especially the cinemas. Through art they confuse us and blind us to our enslavement. Art adorns our prison walls, keeps us silent and diverted and indifferent.

About the Author

Sannion is a mantis ("diviner") and Orpheoteleste ("specialist in Orphic rites") with over two decades' worth of experience worshiping Dionysos and his retinue of gods and spirits. He is a prolific writer and provocateur who publishes under the pseudonym "H. Jeremiah Lewis."

Also from Nysa Press

Thunderstruck With Wine: The Hymns of Sannion

The recitation of hymns during festivals, temple rites and domestic cultus is an ancient part of Hellenic and Italian religion. Collections of hymns circulated under the names of some of the greatest poets – Orpheus, Mousaios, Homer, Pindar, Theokritos, Kallimachos, Proklos and the emperor Julian to name just the best known. And now there are the Hymns of Sannion. This corpus of 31 poems honoring the god Dionysos in his multitude of forms is being published so that contemporary polytheists (be they of his own emergent Bacchic Orphic tradition or not) will have another devotional tool at their disposal. These hymns can be read in their entirety in one sitting or spread out with one read each day of the month. These aren't just poetry filled with lovely imagery and sentiment – they are Keys that open the Labyrinth, letting Dionysos and his mad retinue through into our world. Use them accordingly and carefully.

Heart of the Labyrinth

The Bacchic Orphic spiritual tradition is a complex tapestry woven of many historical threads – Greek, Cretan, Thracian, Egyptian, Italian, Sicilian. Having arisen within these various religions, it also transcends them, just as its foremost god Dionysos transcends all boundaries. Primarily a cult of ecstasy, its adherents seek to bring about release, purification and revitalization through music, dance, ritual drama, feasting, sacrifice and direct communion with the divine. Intentional, ritualized madness, in service of the god, inoculates against more destructive madness. The tradition's strong chthonic focus fosters deep engagement with and reverence for the Dionysian dead – those feasting heroes and furious hunters – for its initiates will one day take their place among those potent spirits. Sannion guides the reader along the winding path of Bacchic Orphism much as he himself discovered it after decades Dionysian worship. Through essays which seamlessly combine primary source material with personal experiences, and poetry that exposes the raw, bleeding heart of devotion and the madness of following a mad god, Sannion explains and explores the living form of this ancient tradition. If you've ever felt the call of Dionysos - and of the gods, heroes and spirits who share his world - this book will help you deepen both your knowledge and devotion, and give you a glimpse into the mysteries of the god who dwells at the Heart of the Labyrinth.

Strange Spirits (Volume One)

A collection of poetry and other mysteries.

Ecstatic: For Dionysos

For a significant portion of his life H. Jeremiah Lewis has struggled to understand the ways and nature of this elusive ancient Greek deity of wine, vegetation, madness, drama, liberation and much else besides. In the course of his study and explorations he has produced an immense body of writing which has been gathered together in this unique volume for the first time ever. In addition to learning about Dionysian history, mythology, symbolism, and methods of worship both ancient and modern, the reader will gain a first-hand glimpse of what it's like to know and love a god as strange as Dionysos.

From the Satyr's Mouth: Wit and Wisdom from an Opinionated Polytheist

In ancient Greece, satyrs were famed for their mocking criticism of societal conventions. H. Jeremiah Lewis brings that same spirit to a discussion of contemporary Pagan life and values in this latest collection of essays.

Prepare to be challenged, informed, annoyed and hopefully entertained!

The Balance of the Two Lands

This collection of essays explores the long history and contemporary manifestations of Greco-Egyptian poly-theism. It provides an overview of the system, information on theology, ethics, the afterlife, and material on domestic worship, ritual forms, and the basics needed to begin practicing today. This is a book for all who have heard the call of the gods of Greece and Egypt and wondered what to do next.

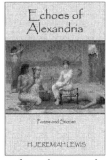

Echoes of Alexandria: Poems and Stories

This volume of poetry and short stories celebrates the author's undying love for the incomparable city of dreamers and the immortal gods and famous historical figures who once walked Alexandria's fabled streets. It offers a unique glimpse into the religious life of a man dedicated to a rich multicultural pantheon drawn from Greece, Egypt, Rome and the Near East. Included are hymns, poetry, imaginative retellings of ancient stories, and modern myths set down for the first time.

Gods and Mortals: New Stories of Hellenic Polytheism

These are the stories of Hellenismos today. What it feels like to recognize the presence of the gods around you. To discover the mystery of the divine, the joy of love, the struggle with doubt, the loneliness of belonging to a minority faith. You can read about ancient Greek religion in academic tomes, but none will tell you what it's like from the inside. The only way to do that is to hear our stories, in our own words. Stories of gods and mortals.

Made in United States
Orlando, FL
27 February 2022

15157562R870089